Parenting Teenage Boys

10 Key Topic to Discuss With Your Teenage Son in Today's World

Rebecca Flag

© Copyright 2022 - All rights reserved.

The content contained within this book may not be reproduced, duplicated or transmitted without direct written permission from the author or the publisher.

Under no circumstances will any blame or legal responsibility be held against the publisher, or author, for any damages, reparation, or monetary loss due to the information contained within this book, either directly or indirectly.

Legal Notice:

This book is copyright protected. It is only for personal use. You cannot amend, distribute, sell, use, quote or paraphrase any part, or the content within this book, without the consent of the author or publisher.

Disclaimer Notice:

Please note the information contained within this document is for educational and entertainment purposes only. All effort has been executed to present accurate, up to date, reliable, complete information. No warranties of any kind are declared or implied. Readers acknowledge that the author is not engaged in the rendering of legal, financial, medical or professional advice. The content within this book has been derived from various sources. Please consult a licensed professional before attempting any techniques outlined in this book.

By reading this document, the reader agrees that under no circumstances is the author responsible for any losses, direct or indirect, that are incurred as a result of the use of the information contained within this document, including, but not limited to, errors, omissions, or inaccuracies.

Table of Contents

INTRODUCTION 1
   HAVING A SON IS COOL... UNTIL HE TURNS INTO A TEENAGER! 1

CHAPTER 1: PUBERTY! AN EXCITING YET CHALLENGING PHASE OF TEENAGE HOOD 3
   UNDERSTANDING THE EMOTIONAL AND PHYSICAL CHANGES BOYS EXPERIENCE DURING PUBERTY 3
      Puberty and Teenage Boys 4
      The Emotional Side of Puberty 10
      In Closing 16

CHAPTER 2: SEX AND TEENAGE BOYS 17
   TALKING ABOUT SEX WITH YOUR TEENAGE SON 17
      Everything Your Teenager Needs to Know About Sex! 18
      Practicing Safe Sex for Teenagers 21
      Tips to Help You Talk to Your Teenager About Sex–Without Embarrassing Them 26
      In Closing 29

CHAPTER 3: FALLING INTO BAD FRIENDSHIPS 31
   PEER PRESSURE AND ITS CONSEQUENCES 31
      Peer Pressure and Dealing With Toxic Friends 32
      What to Do When Your Teenager Is Involved With Bad Friends 41
      In Closing 48

CHAPTER 4: PRIORITIZING MENTAL HEALTH 49
   TEENAGE DEPRESSION AND ANXIETY FOR BOYS 49
      Teenagers and Mental Health 50
      Teenage Depression and Suicide 54
      Strategies Parents Can Use to Bring their Teenagers Out of Depression 58
      In Closing 65

CHAPTER 5: SELF CONFIDENCE FOR TEENAGE BOYS 67
   WHY IT'S IMPORTANT TO LOVE YOURSELF 67
      Teenage Boys and Their Fluctuating Self-Esteem 68
      Overcoming Shame as a Teenage Boy 74
      In Closing 79

CHAPTER 6: SCHOOL MIGHT SUCK, BUT YOU NEED IT! 81

THE IMPORTANCE OF BEING EDUCATED AND HAVING GOALS 81
    Why Do Education and Goal-Setting Matter? 82
    In Closing 88

CHAPTER 7: ADDRESSING ADDICTIVE BEHAVIORS 89

ALCOHOL, SMOKING, DRUGS... AND EVEN GAMING! 89
    Addictive Behaviors in Teenage Boys 89
    Understanding the Seriousness of Gaming Addiction 96
    In Closing 101

CHAPTER 8: DEALING WITH CONFLICT CONSTRUCTIVELY 103

HELPING YOUR TEENAGER MANAGE THEIR ANGER IN TROUBLESOME SITUATIONS 103
    Teenage Boys Are Well-Known For Their Bad Temper 103
    The Consequences of Poor Conflict Management 106
    Strategies to Help Your Teen Deal With Conflict Effectively 109
    In Closing 112

CHAPTER 9 : DATING ADVICE AND LESSONS IN CHIVALRY 115

HOW TO TALK TO YOUR TEENAGE SON ABOUT DATING AND BEING THE PERFECT GENTLEMAN
.... 115
    The World of Dating for Teenage Boys 116
    Dating Advice for Your Teenage Son in the Era of Social Media 120
    In Closing 125

CHAPTER 10: BONDING WITH YOUR TEENAGER 127

FOUR AMAZING BONDING ACTIVITIES FOR YOU TO DO WITH YOUR TEENAGER 127
    1.   Communication Building: Getting to Know One Another 127
    2.   Trust Building: Walking Blindfolded 128
    Empathy Building: Appreciating Perspectives 129
    Bonding Exercise: Have Fun Together! 130
    In Closing 132

CONCLUSION 135

REFERENCES 139

    IMAGE REFERENCES 141

Introduction

Having a Son is Cool… Until He Turns Into a Teenager!

Parents, hear me when I say that having a son is one of the most incredible gifts God could ever give you. They are playful, energetic, easy to dress, and fun to hang out with, but with just a blink of an eye, they go from being high-spirited toddlers to moody teenagers! Most parents are left completely clueless by the time their sons reach teenage hood, and they have no idea what to expect from this new phase of their children's lives even though they have gone through the same experience. When this happens, the million-dollar question arises, which leaves parents scratching their heads in utter confusion: "Why is my child so different?" This, in turn, prompts other questions that parents find themselves pondering: "How can I help my son through this?" and "What can I do to reconnect with my son?"

Raising a teenager is a hard job, so if you think you had it tough when your son was a baby, you got a whole new challenge coming your way. Those terrible twos and daring threes are nothing compared to how much a teenager can test your patience once they reach adolescence, and most boys fall into dangerous, addictive habits because they often feel misunderstood by their parents, and by the world. This is any parent's worst nightmare, because the thought of not being able to help your son when he is going through this phase drives many parents to the brink of insanity, and they often become overprotective and unreasonable in their parenting. The truth is, raising a teenager is an experience that must be embraced to the fullest. You, as a parent, have much to learn from this journey, and there are going to be moments where you feel as though you can't go on. This is when you have to hold on tighter than ever, because your son depends on you.

This book is going to open your eyes to what it's like being a teenager. You're probably thinking that you've already been there, so you know what to expect for your son. However, the world is no longer the same as it was when you were going through your adolescence journey. All the advice, support, and information you need on the various aspects of teenage hood, you will find in this book! Parenting doesn't end when you think that your child is old enough to dress themselves, or sleep alone with the lights off. You have to fulfill your duty as a parent until your son turns 18, and even after that, in some ways. Console yourself, and ease your anxieties even if your job as a parent is not yet complete. There is a sea full of joy to look forward to, and many memories to create with your teenage son! Don't let the fears and doubts of teenage hood scare you away from building a strong relationship with your child. Are you ready to embark on this incredible journey through adolescence? By the time you reach the end of this book, you will be able to understand your son better, approach every situation with love and patience, encourage and support your child through their mistakes, and answer their questions or concerns about anything they are struggling with.

Chapter 1:
Puberty! An Exciting Yet Challenging Phase of Teenage Hood

Understanding the Emotional and Physical Changes Boys Experience During Puberty

In this chapter, you will be exposed to the different changes your teenage son will go through on his journey from childhood into adulthood. Called "teenage hood," this is one of the most challenging phases of a boys' life. This chapter will help answer many of the questions that are plaguing your mind as a parent, and it will serve as a support guide through your parenting journey.

Puberty and Teenage Boys

Puberty is the time in a child's life when they start to mature into young adults. It is known as a rite of passage which bridges the gap between childhood and manhood. There are several changes that take place during this time—both emotional and physical. It's important to understand that these changes do not happen all at once at the same time. Gradually, as time goes by, different changes take place at various stages of puberty. Some boys don't even realize that their body has been going through changes, while others are very aware of the physical and emotional changes that are taking place within themselves. Puberty can be a very confusing time for many teenagers, especially for boys. If it can be this confusing for your son, imagine how confusing it can be for you as a parent! You can help your son get through this phase only if you are able to understand puberty. Fear not! There is much knowledge to be gained from this chapter, and soon you will be able to teach your son everything he needs to know about puberty.

Liam's Puberty Experience

Liam is a 15-year-old boy who started his journey through adolescence when he turned 12. He didn't quite understand what was going on at first, and there wasn't much information about puberty being discussed at school because most teachers assumed it was too early to talk about it. Liam first noticed an itch in his groin area that would come and go, and this irritated him a lot. One day, he decided to look in the mirror to find out what was causing that itch. To his bewilderment, Liam noticed a multitude of tiny hairs growing around his genitals. He couldn't fathom the "how" or the "why" of the whole discovery, and he felt too ashamed to talk to his dad about it. At school, Liam asked one of his friends whether they have experienced the same hair growth, but none of his friends could relate.

This made Liam feel awkward and different from everyone else. The hair growth was only the beginning of many other changes that were taking place in Liam's body. A few weeks later, Liam noticed his voice had started sounding more gruff and hoarse. At first, he thought that he had come down with the flu, but this change in his voice seemed permanent. When Liam turned 13, one of the most confusing and embarrassing changes began taking place. He would get random erections, which increased in frequency as the weeks went by. Liam couldn't understand why this was happening, so he decided to talk to his father about it. He expressed his concerns and shared all the other physical changes that were happening to him with his father.

Liam's father helped him understand that puberty had begun earlier in his case, and he shouldn't feel weird about himself just because his friends started a bit later in their puberty journey. This advice and support from his dad made him feel a lot better about himself, because he finally realized that all the changes he was experiencing are normal for boys who have reached adolescence. The more Liam learned about puberty, the easier it became for him to embrace his new body. Parents need to be extra vigilant when their sons turn 12 and 13 years of age because this is when puberty begins. There are different stages in puberty, with various changes taking place at each stage. Let's take a deeper look at this in the next section.

The Puberty Timeline: Stages of Puberty For Boys

Facial hair, a crackling voice, and acne—boy oh boy, here comes puberty! Teenagers go through a series of changes that take place at different stages in adolescence. While the timing may vary from teenager to teenager, the stages of development, however, should be the same. These developments can cause a lot of discomfort and shame to many teenage boys because they aren't familiar with what's going on inside their bodies. Similar to girls, boys will experience many physical changes that can be hard to understand. These growth spurts and developments are causing changes to their appearance, to their thoughts, and to their lifestyles—which can be a lot to adjust to. Let's take a look at the various stages that puberty is broken down into below.

Stage One: What's Going on Behind the Scenes of Puberty

Before the actual signs of puberty show up, there are other changes taking place behind the scenes. Internal changes are often difficult to point out because a lot of them involve changes with the brain first before they actually show up in the body. Both boys and girls experience these internal changes before puberty begins because it prepares the mind and the body through setting the right environment for those developments that come with puberty. The internal changes which occur are summarized below in point form.

- The brain is an integral part of the whole process as it is solely responsible for preparing the body for puberty by sending signals which alert the body to start developing. Prior to this process, the brain needs to equip and prepare itself for puberty as well.

- Inside the brain, the hypothalamus begins to release a hormone called gonadotropin into the pituitary glands, which will then create different hormones to control other glands in the body.

- The two hormones developed during this time by the pituitary glands are the follicle stimulating hormone (FSH), which helps with sperm production in males and ovary production in females, and the luteinizing hormone (LH), which affects the testes.

- These are all biological changes that are taking place inside the body, so it cannot be seen just yet. As your teenager approaches the next level of puberty, these changes will gradually become visible on the outside of the body.

Stage Two: The Physical Development of the Body Begins

For boys, puberty typically begins around the age of 11. One of the first changes takes place in the genital area of a teenage male. The scrotum (testicles) begins to develop during this stage, and the skin around the scrotum becomes bigger and more defined in shape. Another major sign that puberty has hit your teenager is the growth of pubic hair. Yes, this is a huge sign that your little boy is leaving behind his childhood body and entering into adulthood. Fine hairs begin to grow around the scrotum, and it can be quite uncomfortable at first. Parents can encourage good hygiene to prevent any itching or sweating down there;

however, it's too early to start shaving or removing hair from the genital area, so don't advise your teenager to try that.

Stage Three: Physical Changes Which Begin at Age 13

During this stage, your teenager's hormones are working overtime to continue the development that has taken place over the last two stages. The physical changes are more evident in your teenager now than they were previously. In males, there are many new changes which take place during stage three of puberty. Let's go over a few of them below.

- Teenage boys begin to have wet dreams at night which involve ejaculation.
- The penis grows in size as well, along with the testicles.
- Changes in voice show up, and the pitch goes from high to low until it finally cracks.
- Muscles begin to grow and become more defined on the arms and the calves.
- Your teenager will also get much taller, increasing in their height by two to three inches a year.
- There will also be some growth in the breast tissue, which will gradually fade away after a few years.

Stage Four: Puberty Turns Up!

Puberty is at its peak in both males and females during this stage, which generally starts at around age 14. This can be a challenging time for your teenager because he is still trying to make sense of all the other changes that have taken place so far, and now there are more developments showing up! Adjusting to a new body can be a bit uncomfortable, and many boys often feel as if they can't recognize themselves anymore, while others enjoy the "manly" look they now have. Here are some of the new developments to look forward to in this stage of puberty:

- Body hair continues to grow, appearing in the armpits and growing in length and thickness.
- The genital area is still developing and growing, as the testicles get bigger, along with the penis, and the color of the scrotum will also get darker.
- The change in voice becomes a permanent physical attribute for your teenage son.
- Acne will also develop during this stage of puberty.
- The size of your teenager's feet will also grow a few inches as well.

Stage Five: The Final Stage of Puberty

This is the last stage of your teenager's puberty journey! Your teenager would have come a long way, and he is probably familiar with the sudden changes that his body undergoes. This phase of puberty begins at age 15 and lasts till age 16 or 17, and many of your teenager's physical developments mature and become permanent during this stage. There are a number of developments you will notice as a parent, and they will bring about the realization that your son is almost an adult! This can be an emotional time for parents as they find it difficult to let go of the childhood version of their sons. During this stage, your teenager can expect the following changes:

- Their genitals, such as the penis and testicles will reach an adult size by now.
- The growth of facial hair is much thicker and might require most males to consider shaving to keep themselves looking neat.

- Pubic hair is also another development which will reach its peak during this stage in puberty.

- Hair growth on the legs and hands is also possible in some males.

- Their muscles will continue growing, and most teenagers prefer to play sports and exercise, which is great for muscle development.

- Once your teenager reaches the age of 18, they will have grown to their full potential.

The Emotional Side of Puberty

Ask any parent who has gone through puberty with their teenage sons what the hardest part of it all was. There's no doubt that they will all sing the same song, and tell you that the most challenging part of puberty was the constant mood swings and rebellion they had to endure from their teenager. Some parents were even left devastated and heartbroken because they felt like they didn't know who their child was anymore. The emotional side of puberty can be extremely intense for your teenager, and for your family as well. Similar to how the physical body is undergoing all these changes, your teenager's mind is also maturing and developing. This can cause a lot of emotional instability and anger issues in children who are going through adolescence, and it is absolutely important for parents to make sure that they are helping their teenager deal with their emotions in a healthy way.

Understanding How Puberty Influences a Teenager's Emotions

Puberty affects both the mind and the body, so when it comes to young boys who are going through adolescence, the chances of them experiencing intense emotional changes are very high. Although girls are known for their emotional outbursts and tantrums, boys can also feel emotionally overwhelmed during pubescence. This has a lot to do with their crazy hormones which influence their emotional stability. Along with the physical developments which take place during adolescence, your teenager's mind is also evolving and maturing. This can greatly influence their behavior, as well as their ability to make wise decisions. During puberty, there are many triggers that set off emotional rollercoaster episodes in your teenager. Parents should be aware of these triggers so they can prepare themselves to guide and support their teenager through this.

Trigger One: Physical Changes to their Body

Moms, can you remember the time you felt frustrated and insecure because you couldn't fit into that hot pair of jeans? And dads, how did you feel when you realized that you were losing your beautiful head of hair–your crowning glory? If these natural, physical changes had you feeling depressed and emotional as an adult, can you imagine how your teenager would feel with all the physical changes he is going through? Looking back on the physical developments which take place during puberty, it's quite understandable why your teenager would become insecure and emotional about their appearance. The onset of acne, the weird tone of voice, and the changes in appearance can easily overwhelm any teenage boy, causing them to develop insecurities. Low self-esteem can affect a teenager in many ways, which is why it's important that parents always compliment their sons and try to build up their confidence.

Trigger Two: Changes in Relationships and Friendships

Teenagers become different during puberty, and this change affects their relationships with their family members, as well as their friendships with others. As a teenager goes through these emotional developments, they will lose interest in a lot of things they previously enjoyed doing, and as a result, they will also lose a couple of friends along the way. The loss of meaningful relationships and friendships can also trigger emotional dysfunction in teenagers during puberty. Teenagers want to feel accepted into social circles, so when their friendships come to an end, it can have a tremendous impact on their lives forever. As your teenager goes through these different changes during puberty, their friends and peers might break off friendships for a number of reasons. Interests begin to differ, personalities clash, and physical appearance changes–these are just a few reasons why teenagers and their peers grow apart.

Trigger Three: Hormonal Changes During Puberty

Teenagers become extremely sensitive during puberty, and this is all thanks to their raging hormone levels. Common occurrences such as the sudden appearance of a zit on the face can seem like an epic disaster to your teenager! Or when the Xbox game freezes and he starts shouting and throwing stuff because he lost the battle. Your teenager's reaction to these situations are magnified because of his increased sensitivity during adolescence. A lot of parents find it challenging and scary to address these concerns with their teenager because they have no idea how they will react, so they avoid it altogether. Yes, it very much seems like you are walking on eggshells around your teenager, but this shouldn't be a reason to avoid communicating with him. Your son will need that consistent relationship with you, his parents, throughout his puberty journey.

Finding the Right Time to Talk About Puberty With Your Son

Having a conversation with your son about puberty can seem like a daunting task, especially if you're the "mom" who has to do it. It's generally easier for dads to have this talk with their sons because they can relate to the experience. Fathers can understand the emotional and physical changes that take place during adolescence, but there are many single moms out there who have to step up and help their teenage sons through it. This can be somewhat uncomfortable for these moms, so they try to avoid this conversation, and others refuse to accept the fact that their child is journeying into adulthood! Most parents lose track of time, and they miss out on the opportunity to educate their sons about the developments that are going to take place. Whatever your reason may be, it can never be good enough to justify why you don't want to talk to your son about puberty. Let's be realistic–it's your responsibility, as a parent, to teach your child about these different phases of life so they can prepare themselves mentally to embrace these changes.

There are a few signs you can keep an eye out for that will help you identify the right time to educate your son about puberty.

- You notice that your son is becoming more irritable and moody for no apparent reason.
- He might start asking you questions about girls, dating, and sex.
- You notice physical changes in his appearance that begin to set

him apart from childhood.

- He has just turned 9-years-old, and you notice changes.
- Your son has changed his interests and is no longer amused by childish activities.
- You notice that your son has become more mature and is able to make decisions for himself.

These are just a few things to consider if you are confused about when would be the right time to talk to your child. The only way you can recognize these signs in your son is by paying attention to your child on a regular basis. The majority of parents barely even notice these new developments in their son, and this is why they lose out on that golden opportunity to help their teenager understand what is happening to them.

What Can Parents Do to Make the Conversation Less Uncomfortable for their Teenagers?

Boys tend to shy away from discussions about puberty because they find it somewhat embarrassing to be open about certain things with their parents. When your teenager feels uncomfortable or hesitant, it can be rather difficult to get through to them. No matter how much you talk about puberty with your son, it wouldn't make a difference to him until you manage to break down that wall of skepticism and unwillingness. The truth is that teenagers don't entirely trust adults with sensitive information about themselves, especially when it comes to the physical changes that occur with puberty, because they feel as if the adults wouldn't be able to understand. This mistrust can cause your teenager to become closed off, and this isn't good for communication between parent and child. Luckily, there are some things you can do to help ease your teen's discomfort, so he can open himself up and actively participate in discussions about puberty.

- Before you attempt to have a conversation with your son, think about how you felt when your parents were talking to you about puberty. Write down how you felt during that conversation, and make a list of all the ways your parent(s) could have handled that conversation better.

- Now that you have a clear understanding of what could have been done better, open yourself up to be the parent you needed all those years ago. This shift in perspective will help you understand what your teenager needs from you.

- Choose a good time to talk with your teenager. Don't attempt to start a conversation about puberty in public, or around their friends as it can be extremely uncomfortable for your teenager.

- Approach the conversation with a "friendly" voice instead of a "parental" voice. This helps to ease the tension and nervousness that may be brewing behind the scenes from both parties.

- Don't be forceful or pushy about any topics that you want to discuss with your teenager. If you sense that he is uncomfortable, take a few steps back and allow your teenager some space to become comfortable again.

- Remember that your teenager has a voice. Allow him to speak his mind without interrupting, and be supportive of his experiences. Parents these days want to tell their teenagers what they *should* be experiencing, instead of trying to understand what they are *really* going through.

In Closing

Puberty will always be an uncomfortable topic of discussion between parents and children, so the best thing you can do is be real and supportive of your teenagers' experience. At some point in our lives, we have all gone through puberty. Moms and dads were teenagers once, and even though it might be too long for you to remember, there are certain aspects of your adolescent lives which have impacted you so much that it will stay with you forever. Now, your teenager is going through this same phase of life as you once did. The physical developments, the emotional maturity, and the changes in their social lives are a lot to adapt to for a teenager. Parents must be less judgmental and more understanding towards their teenage sons because not everyone handles puberty the same way. Some teenagers breeze through adolescence without so much as a couple of mood swings here and there, whilst others really battle with low self-esteem and mental health issues like depression. Parents, remain vigilant and try your best to educate your teenage son on the various changes that come along with puberty. The most important gifts you can give your teenager during this time are motivation, support, and love.

Chapter 2:
Sex and Teenage Boys

Talking About Sex With Your Teenage Son

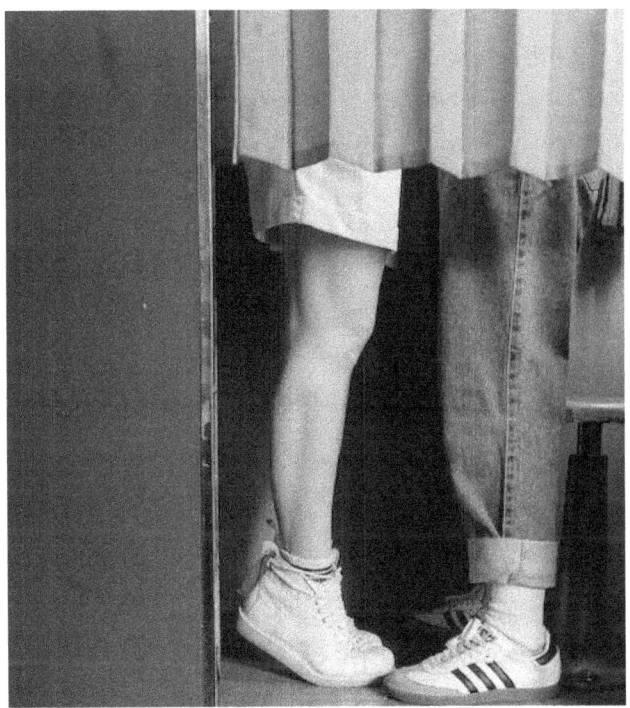

Welcome to the most uncomfortable topic any parent could ever discuss with their teenage son—sex! In this chapter, we aim to help parents shed some light into the world of sex for their teenagers. Everything from when is the right time to talk about sex, to what you can do as a parent to help your child stay safe and abstain from sex for as long as possible, will be discussed in this chapter. So let go of your fears, mom and dad, and get ready to equip yourself with the right tools you need to successfully educate your child about sex.

Everything Your Teenager Needs to Know About Sex!

Millions of parents from around the world all share the same fears when it comes to their teenagers and sex. Yet, it's a topic they avoid talking about as much as they can. The world today has advanced so much that it is next to impossible to hide the idea of sex from your teenager. Whether it's at school, soccer practice, or on social media, your teenager is bound to hear about sex. As much as you try to hide it from them, they are going to pursue the topic of sex with or without your help because teenagers are drawn to the unknown. The last thing a parent wants is for their teenager to explore the world of sex on their own. This is how lifelong mistakes are made and how teenagers land themselves in tricky situations that are hard to get out of.

The Importance of Educating Your Teenager About Sex

Sex is one of the most important aspects of life which your teenager will eventually be exposed to; however, most parents are terrified of educating their teenager about sex because they feel as if they are encouraging them to have sex. While this fear is somewhat justified, it is also, to a certain degree, unfounded. Consider this: When was the last time you or your teenager used algebra in your daily life? Not many times, I assume? See, encouraging your teenager to study is great, but it's also crucial that you teach them about life. Sex is a vital part of life, and no matter how much you try to avoid this topic in your home, your teenager is definitely going to hear about it elsewhere. Understanding the importance of sex education, as a parent, will help you open up and be more forthcoming with information. Here's why it is important to educate your teenage son about sex.

- The right sex education helps prevent your teenager from falling prey to myths and misconceptions about sex, whether from their friends or from what they see on social media.
- Your teenager can make better, more informed decisions when it comes to sex, instead of giving in to their urges.
- Good sex education protects your teenager from sexual abuse and violence. They will be able to tell when someone is being inappropriate with them, which is key to identifying sexual predators.
- If your teenager chooses to engage in sexual activity, sex education will help them practice safe sex, thus preventing sexually transmitted infections and diseases, as well as unwanted pregnancies.
- Parents who are open with their children stand a better chance of influencing their teenager's decisions about sex positively, rather than those parents who avoid the topic, forcing their teenagers to learn about sex on their own.

What Is the True Meaning of Sex?

As parents, the last thing we want is for our teenagers to roam around freely, having sexual intercourse with just about anyone. Although this is very much the culture of the modern world today, it doesn't mean that your teenager should follow this trend. People lack a basic understanding of what sex should be used for, and this skewed perspective results in many unwanted problems. Different people from various cultures all have their own understanding of sex. The Bible is very specific on the topic of sex, and most Christians believe that it is something that should be done only after marriage. The reason for this belief is that sex is an intimate act in which two people join together and become one in the flesh and in the spirit–usually the husband and the wife. Sex is also seen as a way to express your love for your significant other, and to procreate to carry on your lineage.

Nowadays, people have created their own understanding of what sex should be, and it is often void of love and commitment to the other person. One-night stands, casual random hookups, and "friends with benefits" are the new norm when it comes to the sex culture of the twentieth century. Men and women no longer wait until marriage to have sex because they now believe in sexual compatibility. Generally, after the second or third date, sex is introduced into the relationship, and if a person feels dissatisfied, they have a choice to end the relationship. This is a sad reality which has quickly passed down to teenagers, which is why it's so important for parents to teach their children about the true meaning of sex.

The Foundation of Sex

As previously mentioned, Christians believe that sex was created by God for the sole purpose of joining a husband to his wife both physically and spiritually. However, people's carnal desires and fantasies have taken over, obliterating the true meaning of sex in the process. People now use sex as a means of pleasure and control, and they aren't afraid of putting this message out there. The foundation of sex consists of many layers, namely, respect, love, commitment, and promise. As adults, do you really believe that the world is honoring this foundation? Or has it created a new one? Parents, you need to be that voice of reasoning and truth for your teenager who is new to the world of sex. If you can identify the ways in which the world has twisted the once innocent idea of sex into something that is perverse and lustful, you can teach your children right from wrong.

It can be challenging to help your teenager see things from your perspective, especially when they are being influenced by outside opinions. You can try explaining the real meaning of sex in the most straightforward way possible. Help your teenager understand that their body is special and should be protected and looked after, and that they should only give themselves to someone who respects them and loves them genuinely. Your child must realize that their body is connected to their soul, and having multiple sexual partners can destroy the balance and open up doors to all kinds of problems. Yes, sex is very much enjoyable and exciting, but the more often you engage in meaningless sex, the less exciting and pleasurable it can be.

Practicing Safe Sex for Teenagers

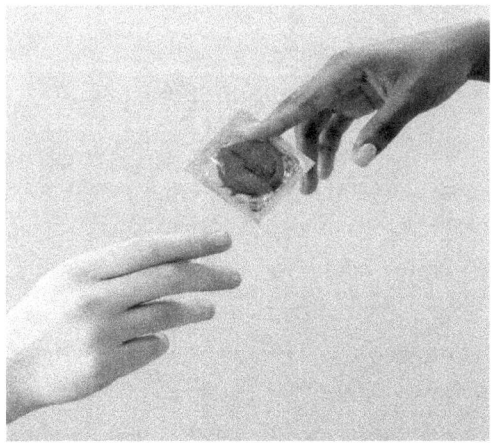

Okay, I get it. Educating teenagers on how to practice safe sex might seem as if you are encouraging them to be sexually active. Sometimes, when parents try to teach their children how important it is to use a condom, or how vital it is that they stick to one sexual partner, their children often get the wrong idea. Just because you are trying to educate your teenager, it doesn't mean you are giving them a free pass to engage in sex! Nonetheless, avoiding this topic isn't going to do you much good either. Parents often find themselves standing at a crossroads, unable to make a decision about whether to talk to their teengers about practicing safe sex. By the time these parents gather the courage to make a decision, their teenagers have already engaged in sexual intercourse many times. In this day and age, it's crucial that parents act fast, and think clearly when it comes to making decisions about their children's lives. Even though you might not like your decision, it's important that you make the right choice for the sake of your teenager. The truth is, no one knows your teenager better than you! Your child is going through the most difficult chapter in their lives, and they won't always make the right choices. It's up to you, as a parent, to do what is best, even if your teenager disagrees with the choice you have made. It's time to talk about practicing safe sex with your son, before it's too late. This section will provide you with the tips and information you need to educate your child about engaging in safe sex and being responsible.

What Does it Mean to Practice Safe Sex?

The term "safe sex" doesn't only refer to being responsible when engaging in sexual activities–it also refers to abstinence. Choosing not to have sex is also a form of being safe, and parents should make this known to their teenagers. Practicing safe sex can seem boring or burdensome to teenagers because they would much rather give in to the pleasures of their body, instead of thinking about doing the right thing. However, once parents educate their teenagers on the consequences of engaging in unprotected sex, they will instantly adopt an understanding for themselves on why it is so important to protect oneself during sex.

Below, you will find the most important topics you can discuss with your teenager about practicing safe sex.

Educating Your Teen on HIV/AIDS

HIV/Aids can be a sensitive topic to talk about with teenagers, especially if you are living in a low to middle income community. In these communities, HIV/Aids isn't just some story you tell to get your kids to stay away from sex—it's a reality people have to live with. Before you attempt to educate your teenage son about HIV/Aids, make sure that you do enough research first. There are many parents who give their children false information about this disease and thus cause or spread confusion. Here are a few facts about HIV/Aids that you can share with your teenager.

- HIV (Human immunodeficiency virus) is a virus which attacks the infection- fighting cells in the human body, thus making the body more prone to infections.
- Aids is the end stage of the HIV infection. This stage occurs when the body's immune system is too weak to fight off any other infections.
- The HIV virus is spread through the exchange of bodily fluids, such as blood and semen, which happens during sexual intercourse, as well as using the same injection equipment, or through an open wound.
- You cannot get HIV just by touching someone, or by hugging or kissing.
- There are medications which have been developed to help minimize the spread of the disease and to help patients live healthy lives.
- HIV can be prevented by using a condom to have safe sex.

- Before you decide to have sexual intercourse with someone, make sure that you are aware of their HIV status.

Educating Your Teen on STDs

Sexually transmitted diseases (STDs) are quite common among youngsters these days. These infections are spread through sexual activity, from person to person, for example, through penetrative vaginal sex, through oral sex, or through anal sex. There are many forms of STDs, and teenagers are prone to these infections because they usually like to experiment at this age, with different forms of sexual activity. Having multiple sexual partners, and engaging in anal sex increases the risk of contracting an STD significantly. Parents might feel uncomfortable talking about oral sex and anal sex with their teenager, but it is a topic that shouldn't be left out of the discussion. Below, you will find a list of the most common STDs.

- **Chlamydia**: This infection is spread during sex, and it can cause a discharge from the penis or vagina, with pain in the lower belly, and fever. It can be cured and prevented with the right medication.

- **Genital Herpes:** This infection is spread through oral or vaginal sex, and it causes sores and lesions to appear on the genital area. This infection cannot be cured, although the outbreaks can be managed with medications. People with genital herpes might not have any symptoms at all, so it is important that you encourage protected sex at all times.

- **Gonorrhea**: This infection is spread through sexual intercourse from someone who already has the infection. It causes a yellowish or greenish discharge from the vagina or the penis, pain and burning when urinating, and a fever. The infection can be cured with effective antibiotics which must be taken over three months.

Educating Your Teen on Birth Control, Condoms, and Teenage Pregnancy

Practicing safe sex also revolves around preventing unwanted pregnancy at a young age. No parent is ever prepared to see their child become parents themselves before they even reach the age of 18. Unfortunately, teenage pregnancy has been rising rapidly over the past few years as teenagers continue to become careless and irresponsible during sex. Whether you believe it or not, there is no concrete way to know whether your teen is sexually active. So the best thing you can do to prevent teenage pregnancy is to educate your son about it. Talk to your teenager about using condoms correctly in order to minimize the risk of pregnancy. There are also other forms of contraceptives which are effective, such as birth control pills, morning-after pills, and female condoms. This conversation will be awkward to say the least, but prevention is better than cure. Suck in all your uncomfortable feelings, and give it to your child straight! Teenage pregnancy is no joke, so your teenage son should be made fully aware of how his actions could dictate the rest of his life. One time is all it takes to get pregnant, so caution is key every time he decides to have sex. The worst mistake any parent can make is assuming that their child isn't going to engage in sexual activity. While your teenager might seem innocent and uninterested in sex, they could be influenced differently by their friends. It's wiser to educate your teenagers at home, rather than leaving them open to outside influence. Some parents feel very uncomfortable talking about these topics with their youngsters. However, armed with confidence and research, you can educate your child about these important aspects of life, and save them from falling prey to STDs and Infections.

Tips to Help You Talk to Your Teenager About Sex– Without Embarrassing Them

Some of the most significant discussions we, as parents, could ever have with our children involve sex and how to be responsible with your body. Sex is a topic often overlooked because it is regarded as taboo to talk about in most households across the world. In countries such as India, China, and South America, among many others, the topic of sex is often avoided. This is due to the "old-fashioned" thinking of strict parents who assume sex is only to be engaged in after marriage. Whilst these parents aren't wrong in their beliefs, it does pose a problem when such beliefs no longer align with reality. Teenagers all over the world are engaging in sexual intercourse from a young age. It's their lack of knowledge about sex that causes their irresponsible behavior, which leads to numerous teenage pregnancies and sexually transmitted diseases. If only these parents woke up and faced reality, and educated their children on sex, then the risk of reckless sexual behavior would be minimized. After all, it is with knowledge that we can protect ourselves and make informed decisions.

Moms and dads, it is your responsibility to shift your thinking from the "old" to the "new" in order to protect your children. Keeping your mindset renewed and in line with the changing world is key to protecting your teenagers and making them aware. I'm sure you must have made your own share of mistakes when you were younger, and one of the main reasons for that is a lack of knowledge or desire to find out for yourself. Now that you have been through those experiences, you are in the right position to make sure that your child doesn't fall into those same traps. Yes, teenagers are stubborn, and no matter how hard you try to guide them, ultimately, they will make their own decisions. But you can be that voice of reasoning and wisdom that makes them wary of the consequences that come with their actions. Below, you will find a couple of helpful tips to help you talk to your teenage son about sex. Use them to your advantage, and don't forget to maintain a level of confidence in yourself as a parent. You are doing the right thing!

Don't Act Like a Know-It-All

Whilst you may be the experienced one in this conversation between parent and child, it would help a lot if you simply stooped down to your teenager's level when talking about sex. Most parents like to preach to their children, and act like they are experts on the topic of sex. This is the worst thing you can do because it instantly makes your teenager turn a deaf ear to everything you have to say. Naturally, teenagers strongly dislike talking to their parents about sex, so they will go into a conversation with the intent to tune out everything you say. The only way you can avoid this is by making yourself humble and approachable during the conversation. Preaching to your teenager isn't going to do him any good.

Be Open and Honest

Believe it or not, teenagers appreciate honesty from their parents! It's one of the most effective ways to gain your child's trust when building a relationship with them. Parents can sometimes hide and twist information when they are uncomfortable talking about it with their teenagers. However, this can cause a lot of indifference and trust issues between parent and child. If your teenager figures out that you have been giving them incorrect information, they will think twice about coming to you for advice in future. Be transparent with your teen, and don't withhold any information about sex. It's better if they hear everything about sex from a parent, rather than hearing it from their friends. When you sit down to have this talk with your son, put aside your parental image for a little while. Think of yourself as a trusted friend who is helping another friend understand everything about sex. This way, you come across less judgmental and more supportive towards your teen.

Create a Tension-Free Atmosphere

Most parents prefer having "the talk" with their teenagers at home because it's a safe place where parents can be open with their children. However, things have changed a lot over the years, and teenagers have become demanding and less understanding. Consider taking your teenager out for a walk at the park, or for ice cream at the mall to create a bonding experience before you have the actual conversation. Parents have to work a little harder to reconnect with their teenagers before talking to them about sensitive topics like sex. The reality is, your teenager is drifting a little further away from you every day. All of their time is consumed by smartphones, hanging out with friends, watching TV, and playing sports. Teenagers rarely have time for their parents, and this can cause a disconnect in their relationship. So, when a parent wants to have a meaningful conversation with their child, there is immediate hesitation because the parent doesn't know how their teen will react. The only way you can get rid of this hesitation is by setting the right atmosphere to have a talk with your teenage son. Once the distance has been bridged, everything else will flow smoothly in conversation.

Encourage Questions

Teenagers are basically children who are growing into adulthood. They have little to no knowledge about sex, except for what they hear from others or see on TV. During your discussion with your teenager, encourage him to ask questions about anything he doesn't fully understand. The whole aim of talking to your teen about sex is to educate him so he can be responsible and make better decisions. This is only possible if he understands everything you have been teaching him.

Asking questions is a great way to clear up any doubts that your teenager might have in his mind about sex. For instance, you could be teaching your son about practicing safe sex with a condom, but he has heard from his friend that sex is better without one. You, as a parent, wouldn't know about this unless you asked questions, and encouraged your son to do the same. The more your teenager understands about sex, the less chance of him making mistakes.

In Closing

Parents, it is well understood that you don't want your teenager engaging in sex this early on in their lives. Fearing that your child is out there having sex is any parent's worst nightmare! But ask yourself, "Why am I so afraid? Where is this fear coming from?" Soon, you will find out the answers to those questions. You don't necessarily fear the fact that your teenager is having sex, but you fear the consequences of their actions. What if your teenager exposes himself to an STD? What if he makes a girl pregnant? These "What If" questions spark fear in you, causing you to become stressed and paranoid. There is a very simple solution to this problem of yours: equipping your teenager with all the knowledge he needs to be responsible sexually. This chapter has provided you with amazing skills you need to talk to your teenager freely, without any hesitation or anxiety. Keep in mind that educating your teenager on sex doesn't mean that you are encouraging them to become sexually active. Parents should make this point clear to their teens before and after having the conversation. At the end of the day, mom and dad, your adolescent son is going to make his own decisions. You can remain calm, knowing that you did your part and fulfilled your responsibility of imparting knowledge to your child. As parents, all we can do is guide and educate our children– the rest is up to them.

Chapter 3:
Falling into Bad Friendships

Peer Pressure and Its Consequences

This chapter aims to help parents understand the dangers of peer pressure, and realize how it can negatively impact their teenagers' lives in the long run. Parents are more experienced with life and relationships, so they can prepare their teenagers to be wary of friends who are a bad influence in their lives. By the end of this chapter, you will be able to understand how friendship works from a teenage boy's perspective, and how bullying and peer pressure are common in schools and among friends these days.

Peer Pressure and Dealing With Toxic Friends

Have you ever felt the need to do something just because everyone else was doing it? For instance, your neighbor down the road invites you over to their famous Sunday barbeque, and when you arrive there, you notice that everyone is drinking, even though they have to work the next day. At the back of your mind, you know that you shouldn't be drinking because you have to stay fresh for that meeting in the morning, but everyone else urges you to have just one drink since it wouldn't make much of a difference. You hear Reggie telling you how boring you are just because you didn't want to drink on a Sunday, so you eventually decide to have a drink just to shut them up. However, one drink turns into four, and soon you realize that it's too late–you're already drunk. Just as Bob, a grown 40-year-old man, made you feel dull because you didn't want to drink, so do teenagers sometimes make each other feel lame because of their choices. Peer pressure exists no matter how old you are, and parents need to teach their children that it is not cool to do things to please other people.

What Is Peer pressure?

Simply put, peer pressure is choosing to do something you wouldn't otherwise do, usually because you want to feel accepted by your social circle. Teenagers are prone to peer pressure the most because of their vulnerability and willingness to follow the behaviors of their friends, especially when it comes to fitting in and finding their click at school. No teenager wants to feel like an outcast, so they do whatever it takes to prove to their peers that they are worthy of being accepted into a group. Peer pressure can be either positive or negative, depending on the type of people you join. However, negative peer pressure seems to be the most common type of peer pressure you will find among teens these days. Every teenager has been growing up in their own way, with their own set of values instilled in them by their parents. These values can sometimes clash when teenagers look for their place in the social circle because some of them might be okay with drinking alcohol and having sex at an early age, while others believe that they should abstain from these activities until they are of an appropriate age.

Peer pressure kicks in when teenagers have to compromise on their values and participate in certain activities just so they can gain approval and recognition from the teenagers who are deemed "cool" in their group. This places an extremely large amount of pressure on youngsters, who feel they have to compromise just to fit in. A teenager's inability to say no to others is what places them in a position to become negatively influenced by their peers. There are different levels to peer pressure, and parents should pay close attention to the changes they notice taking place with their teenagers. A sudden change in their taste in music, or in the way your teen dresses isn't much of a cause for concern. Parents will know when to take their teenagers' behavior seriously, especially when they notice that it's out of the ordinary.

What Peer Pressure Looks Likes for Teenagers

Teenagers have a hard enough life as it is with all the changes they are going through because of puberty. Then comes peer pressure, with all of its influence and power to destroy a teenager's future. Peer pressure always goes unnoticed because the majority of the time, these adolescent boys don't even realize that they are being coerced or forced by their friends to behave in a certain manner that goes against their values. If your teenager finds himself in a situation where he feels compelled to do something he is uncomfortable with, he would simply brush it off as his friends urging him to do this because they want him to fit in the group, or to be cool like the rest of them. Not for one minute would he consider the fact that his friends are being manipulative and selfish for their own gain and entertainment.

Due to a lack of information on peer pressure, many teenagers have no clue what they are dealing with. How can they stand up for themselves, or break away from toxic friends when they aren't even aware that they are being forced to compromise on their values? Parents, this is where you come in. It is your responsibility to help your teenager navigate their friendships in a supportive way.

Signs of Peer Pressure in Teenagers

Teenagers are pros at hiding things from their parents, especially when it comes to the mischief they are getting up to with their friends. Since most parents hardly ever sit down and have a good conversation with their teenagers, they easily miss out on the signs that their child might be exposed to peer pressure. There are several reasons why teenagers choose to hide their feelings from their parents–from– the fear of being embarrassed in front of their friends to feeling like their parents won't understand the situation they are in. Whatever the reason for it, peer pressure should never be ignored. Here are the signs you should look out for, indicating that your teenager is being bullied into doing things they are not comfortable with.

- Increased aggressiveness and frequent mood swings.
- Loss of interest in the things they loved doing.
- Spending a lot of time on their own, often locking themselves in their rooms.
- Avoiding certain friends by not answering their calls or meeting up with them, and refusing to talk about them.

- A change in eating habits, such as loss in appetite, or eating more than usual.
- Being hesitant to go to school and making excuses to stay at home.
- Changes in their sleep patterns: oversleeping, not getting enough sleep, and having frequent nightmares.
- Asking you for pocket money all the time.
- Their belongings, such as their phones, laptops, watches, clothing and shoes, are either going missing or being destroyed in some way.
- They have become more distant and secretive lately, and they don't like answering questions that are directed at their friendships.
- They seem depressed and anxious all the time.

These are some of the signs parents should keep an eye out for. Although these signs could easily be explained away by a number of different things, peer pressure should always be included in the top three list. When it comes to raising teens, parents should be extra vigilant and alert towards any changes in their behavior. It's shocking just how fast your child could change under the influence of their friends. Understanding the difference between good friends and bad is key to helping your child stay away from bullies and fake friends.

Positive Friends vs Negative Friends: How to Help Your Teenager Identify Friendships

Making friends is an important part of your teenager's development. Puberty can be a very confusing and intense phase in your teen's life, so bonding with other teenagers who are experiencing the same changes in life helps make the process much easier and tolerable. While making friends is a crucial aspect of every teenager's life, it's also important that they choose the right type of friends who can influence them positively. Friendship is essential to every human being's life, no matter how old or young they may be. However, choosing the right type of friends can be very difficult for teenagers because they have no experience in judging other people's intentions. This is where parents can draw on their life experience to help guide their children. I know what you are probably thinking–your teenager will never listen to a word of advice you have to offer him, but whether he likes it or not, you are the experienced one.

Sooner or later, your teenager will come to you for advice regarding his friendships. It can be hard to distinguish positive friends from negative ones even for adults. So, unless you develop a good understanding between the two, you wouldn't be able to advise your teenager. Everyone feels the need to be accepted, to have a circle of friends they belong to in life. But there are consequences of choosing the wrong type of people as friends. Below, we take a closer look at how you can identify positive friendships and negative ones. Once you, as a parent, can recognize key differences between the two, you will be able to guide your teenager down the right path. You can also use the information given below, to help your teen gain their own understanding of positive vs negative friendships.

What Do Positive Friendships Look Like?

Before you can ask yourself what a positive friendship looks like, consider asking yourself this question first: What does friendship mean? Friendship can mean different things to different people, especially when they don't have a proper understanding of what it really is. The most basic understanding of friendship is being able to share your sorrows and joys with someone who encourages you to become the best version of yourself. Not everyone is able to grasp the true meaning of friendship, which is why it's so hard to find good friends these days. You can help your teenager find good friends, and become a good friend themselves, through guidance and support.

If your teenager develops an understanding of what positive friendship looks like from a young age, he will be able to choose the right friends and save himself a lot of trouble in the process. There are a couple of major points to look out for when trying to identify the positive friends in your life. Here are a few of them.

- A good friend shares in your happiness and sadness, and they always seem to add joy to your life.

- Whenever you are feeling less confident in yourself, a good friend will remind you of your strengths and capabilities to help boost your confidence.

- A good friend is always there whenever you need their help, and they will never turn a blind eye when you are in trouble.

- If you are going astray, a positive friend will bring you back onto the right path by pointing out your wrong actions and motivating you to do the right thing.

- A good friend is neither jealous nor envious of your achievements. They will always celebrate with you, no matter where they are in their lives.

- You never feel pressured or forced by your friend into doing anything you don't want to do. They respect your choices and allow you to make your own decisions.

The points mentioned above are all indicative of a strong, healthy friendship which takes effort and commitment from all parties involved. If you want to find a true friend in your life, you must be willing to be a true friend as well. You cannot expect all of this from someone if you are not willing to offer the same in return. A healthy friendship works both ways. If your teenager wants to attract positive friends into his life, he must be willing to have a positive mindset and attitude. When your teenager feels happy and uplifted whenever he is with his friends, that's how he will know if he has chosen the right people to be around.

What Do Negative Friendships Look Like?

Sometimes, it can be difficult to notice when negative people have entered your life disguised as friends. At first, they will seem as if they have your best interests at heart so they can gain your trust, and once they see that they can manipulate you, there's no telling what they are capable of doing. Believe it or not, teenagers are very capable of being manipulative and toxic. You might think that only adults have the ability to use people and take advantage of others, but teenagers can do the same thing to get what they want. As a parent, you want to do everything you can to protect your child from being influenced negatively and treated badly by the people they trust. But it can be a challenge to warn your teenagers of toxic friends, especially when they have been blinded by the "friendship bomb." Toxic friendships are generally the most difficult friendships to get out of because the victim always gets sucked back in by those friends who make life seem exciting. The desire to become popular, to find a place where they feel accepted can sometimes take over your teenager's ability to think clearly, and this is why they often fall into the traps set by their negative peers.

The key to helping your teenager stay clear of toxic friendships is to educate them on the signs to look out for that will help them spot a negative person from a mile away. The more your teenager understands about how the world works, the better for them because they can recognize when to keep their guard up and when to let it down. Having a toxic friend in your life manifests in many ways that will raise red flags in your mind. If you suspect that your teenager has been hanging out with the wrong company, it's important that you take action as soon as you can. Here are some signs you can keep an eye out for as they indicate your teenager has negative friends.

- Whenever your teenager comes back home from hanging out with his friends, he may seem irritable and upset. You will notice how his moods are when he leaves the house, compared to when he returns home.

- If your teenager needs help with a project, or with something in his personal life, his friends are nowhere to be seen. They don't return his calls, or come over to check in on him.

- The only time your teenagers' friends will contact him is if they need something from him. Whether it's a ride to school, or help with schoolwork—the only time they can be seen is when they need his help.

- These friends become jealous of your teenager's achievements, and they refuse to celebrate with him on his good days.

- Your teenager feels forced or coerced to do certain things, and he has a hard time saying no to these friends because he is afraid of what might happen if he does.

- You notice that your teenager is losing his self-confidence and doesn't want to hang out with these friends anymore.

- These toxic friends often insult or make fun of your teenager in public to make themselves look good.

When it comes to identifying negative peers as a teenager, it takes a huge event to occur before you can begin to see things for yourself. That's how teenagers learn about others, and about life, by making mistakes and trusting the wrong people. Parents, if your teenager refuses to accept your advice when it comes to breaking away from toxic friends, let them continue with the friendship. Eventually, your teenager will see the true side of their friends. Allow them to make these mistakes so they can learn from them. However, if you want to try harder to get your message across, you will need expert advice on how to talk to your teenager about negative friends.

What to Do When Your Teenager Is Involved With Bad Friends

If you are a concerned parent who wants to talk to your teenager about the friendships they are committing to, you will need to keep all lines of communication open and accessible with your child before you try to have this conversation with them. Teenagers rarely trust their parents when it comes to making decisions about their friendships. One of the main reasons for this is that they feel that their parents are too old to understand how friendships work in the new generation. You heed to reassure your teenager that despite your age, you have experience when it comes to identifying toxic people.

Helping Your Child Recognize Negative Friendships

Parents have struggled with getting their teenagers away from those friends who have a negative influence over their lives. This might seem like an easy task, especially when you think that your teenager is going to listen to you just because you are the parent. However, teenagers are quick to defend their friendships at any cost. While you might see a child who is insolent and badly behaved, your teenager sees the exact opposite when it comes to their friends. This conflict of opinion could end up pushing your teenager further away from you. Here's how you can handle the situation differently.

Don't Badmouth Your Child's Friends

I think we all can agree that talking bad about someone else gets you nowhere. The worst mistake any parent can make is to badmouth their teenager's friends in an attempt to break off the friendship. Parents, think back to those years when you were a teenager. I'm sure your mother or father must have given you an earful about joining a certain type of friend. In your parents' eyes, this friend of yours was bad news, and they wanted you to stay as far away as possible from this person. Did you listen to your parents back then? Or did you continue running around with this friend on the down low? Teenagers see things from their own perspective, and oftentimes this causes a conflict of opinion between parent and child. As long as your teenager doesn't agree with what you are thinking or saying, they will never do what you have asked them to do. The key to opening your teenager's eyes lies with gaining their trust. The moment you have something bad to say about their friends, that is when your teenager will cease to trust you.

Verbally insulting and attacking your child's friends will only paint you as the villain in their story. Your teenager will automatically think that you are being judgmental and dismissive of their friends because you want to control them. You can get your message across to your child without speaking poorly of their friends. When you try to explain things in a decent manner, your child won't be so quick to defend their friends, or to shut down your opinions.

Make a Genuine Effort to Get to Know Your Teenager's Friends

Human beings are always quick to judge others based on what they see or hear, instead of getting to know a person first. When it comes to your child, getting to know their friends is an important aspect of parenting. Most parents these days don't take the initiative to spend some time with their teenager's friends. They simply allow them to make friends with whoever they want, whenever they want. The heart of the problem lies with the parents who fail to realize that their teenagers spend at least 80% of their time with these friends. The amount of trust that builds up between these friends within that time can't be undone overnight. If you want to get your child to see things from your perspective, you will have to show them that you're making an effort to get to know their friends.

If you had to ask your child to stay away from a friend, their first response to you would be, "But you don't even know them!" Your teenager would get the impression that you are judging their friends without even getting to know them. It's also wise, as an adult, to learn as much as you can about someone before forming an opinion about them. This is a good lesson to teach your teenager as well. Judging someone without understanding who they are and where they come from is unfair and unjust.

Teach Your Child About True Friendship

Because teenagers are so young and naive, they have no clue as to what good friendships should look like. They easily get caught up in their own worlds, thinking that they have formed lifelong friendships with the best people. While this may be true for a few of their friends, there are also those teenagers who disguise themselves as true friends but they don't really care all that much about their friendships. Your son could become involved with these kinds of teenagers who bullies others and takes advantage of them. Before you jump down your teenager's throat about the kind of friends he is keeping, consider teaching him about genuine friendships so that he can see the reality of his friendships for himself. As parents, we are always quick to shout and reprimand our children about making poor decisions, but we don't take the time to teach them the right things so that they can make good choices for themselves. If you talk to your child from a young age about friendships, they will grow up to choose the right kind of people to call their friends, because they have been taught critical skills on how to identify good friendships.

Introduce Your Teenager to Positive Youngsters Who Share Similar Interests

Eventually, there will come a time when you are tired of arguing with your teenager about their friendships. Talking to them would seem pointless, so the best thing you can do is show them what they're missing out on. Consider introducing your son to other teenagers who are more ambitious, optimistic, positive, and grounded in their values. There are many ways you can do this, so don't stress yourself out wondering how you are going to make this happen. Enroll your teenager in extracurricular activities outside of school, such as swimming classes, dancing, sports, volunteering at charity organizations, and bible studies.

Host a party at home and invite those teenagers you feel would have a good influence on your son. Parents understand what is good for their children, so steer your child in the direction you want them to go.

Try to Help Your Teenager's Negative Friends Change their Mindsets

Even those toxic friends whom your teenager is involved with deserve to get a second chance. Most parents don't take the initiative to understand why their teenager's toxic friends are that way. Have you ever asked yourself why these teenagers are behaving this way? Why do they get into trouble all the time? I guess you haven't. At the end of the day, these troubled teenagers are still kids themselves. They need proper guidance and support to change their ways. Maybe they are dealing with a difficult home life. There's probably emotional or physical abuse going on, or maybe there is financial trouble in the household. Whatever the reasons may be, these teenagers often act out in ways that are self-destructive.

Writing someone off without giving them a chance to redeem themselves isn't fair. Consider sitting down with your teenager's troubled friends and have a conversation with them about getting some help to change their behavior. Offer to help in any way you can, trying to show them that it's not too late to turn things around for the better. Sometimes, all these teenagers need is for someone to have faith in them.

What Can Parents Do to Help Their Teenager Who is Dealing With Peer Pressure?

If your teenager is dealing with a friend who is pressuring them to do things they don't want to do, then you should take immediate action. In this case, it's your child's life at stake so there's no time to wait for things to settle on their own. Many times, teenagers who are being coerced or forced by their friends to engage in certain activities become involved in underage drinking, smoking, drugs, and sexual behavior. These are all serious issues that have to be dealt with responsibly because they could become a habit that will affect your son for the rest of his life! As a concerned parent, here's what you can do to remove your teenager from that situation.

- Get your teenager to open up about the things they have been forced or influenced to do by being supportive and understanding. Tell your child that you can only help him if you have a good understanding of everything that is going on.
- Visit the school and request a meeting with the parents of the friend who has been bullying or pressuring your child to participate in these activities.
- Allow your teenager to bear the consequences of their actions and accept any punishment handed out to them by the school etc. This will help your teenager realize that he should be responsible for the decisions he makes.
- If your teenager is displaying signs of depression and behavioral issues, consider reaching out to a healthcare professional for help. Book counseling sessions with a therapist or guidance counselor to help your child overcome any mental health issues he has developed as a result of the peer pressure.
- Consider changing schools if your teenager doesn't show any improvement in their demeanor or in their school life. Sometimes, a change of schools might help your teenager get over their PTSD from being bullied or forced into doing things they weren't comfortable with.
- Teach your child how to stand up for themselves, saying "no" to things that go against their own values and beliefs. Build up your teenager's self-confidence so that they refuse to let others take advantage of them and bully them around. The only way your

son is going to overcome peer pressure is by taking a stand against these negative friends who try to manipulate him.

Strategies for Disarming Peer Pressure (For Teenagers)

Here are a few quick, fool-proof strategies that you can teach your teenagers to help them take control of a situation where they might feel pressured by their peers.

1. Ask as many questions as you can. For example, one of your friends is a smoker, and they offer you a puff, saying that it would make you feel less stressed. Ask them why they smoke, how long they have smoked for, and if they feel like it's contributing to their overall health. This will make them rethink their decision to offer you a cigarette in future, and it will make them question their own choice to smoke as well.

2. Say "no" firmly, like you mean it. Maintain eye contact with your friends when you are saying "no," keeping a serious tone of voice. This will send the message across that you are not joking, and they will stop bugging you in future.

3. Remove yourself from the pressure-filled situation. If you are going to remain in the presence of your friends when they are doing things that make you uncomfortable, you're going to feel tempted to give in to them. Take a walk, telling your friends that you will catch up with them later on.

4. Avoid these stressful situations as much as you can. If you know that there is going to be a party where teenagers will be drinking, smoking, and having sex, avoid them. When a teenager is battling with his ability to say "no," he shouldn't be found in situations that are going to overwhelm him.

5. Think about how you are going to feel if you give in to the pressure. Are the guilt and the shame worth it? When you think

about the consequences of your actions, it will help you stand up and say "no" to your friends.

6. Don't be afraid to speak out against bullying and peer pressure. You can be the voice of hope for other teenagers who are going through the same experience. Staying quiet and enduring it all sends the wrong message to the bully, as well as to the other children who are suffering.

In Closing

Peer pressure is a daily problem that many teenagers have to face, and oftentimes they have to face it alone. When your teenager is insecure about himself, he will do whatever it takes to fit in, which includes doing everything their friends ask of them regardless of whether it's right or wrong. Parents will try to do whatever they can to help their children, but if your teenager doesn't stand up for themselves, the peer pressure will continue. This chapter has provided you with some incredible tips on how to help your child when he has chosen bad friendships. They key doesn't lie in arguing or ordering your teenager to quit those friendships. It lies in understanding their friends and building up your teenager's self-esteem so that they can make healthy choices, which benefits them in the long run. If you teach your child what good friendships should be like from a young age, and if you help them build their confidence, your teenager will surely make the right decisions when it comes to choosing their friends. Peer pressure is a phase in every youngster's life, but it only remains a phase if you take action against it.

Chapter 4:
Prioritizing Mental Health

Teenage Depression and Anxiety for Boys

In this chapter, parents will come face to face with the monster called teenage depression that plagues youngsters around the world these days. Mental health problems occur not only in adults, but they also show up in adolescent boys who are experiencing changes to their mind and body during puberty. This chapter will help parents arm themselves with the right strategies to bring their teenagers out of the darkness caused by depression. You will come to understand what depression is, how it is caused, and why it affects teenagers more intensely. The more you learn about mental health, the better equipped you will be to save your teenager from being consumed by it.

Teenagers and Mental Health

Mental health is a topic that has broken all barriers to make itself known in today's society. Previously avoided, if not ignored, by many people, depression and mental health have drawn more attention and interest from researchers over the last few years. Since Covid-19 emerged and the lockdown was issued, millions of people have reported that they are suffering from various mental health disorders, such as anxiety, PTSD, depression, and behavioral disorders. People are finally voicing their concerns, opening up about their struggles, and seeking help because they understand how important it is to take care of your mental health. On the other hand, there has been a rise in the number of cases in teenage suicide around the world. It has become a real concern for parents who have teenagers, because they are afraid that their children might become a part of the statistics. Millions of parents have found themselves wondering, "Why is my teenager so depressed?" The truth is, there could be a number of reasons why a teenager might be depressed, but one of the most common reasons is the big "P"—puberty!

Trigger Warning

Austin's Emotional Journey Through Puberty

Austin was the type of boy who loved spending time with his family. Ever since he could remember, he would climb onto his mother's bed at night and snuggle up with her, placing his head on her warm, jelly-like tummy. He was breastfed as a baby, so he often craved that warmth of being close to his mother's skin. Even when Austin turned 13-years-old, he would still find comfort in his mom by laying his head on her tummy at night. This was a beautiful bond they both shared, and Austin's mom loved the fact that no matter how old her son would get, he would still need her the way he did when he was younger. Apart from his bond with his mom, Austin really loved playing with his little sister. They were only two years apart, so they had a lot in common age wise. Austin and his sister would sneak out into the backyard and play with the tadpoles in the pond, and whenever it rained, they would scoop up some of those tadpoles and take them into the house until the rain subsided. These siblings spent almost every minute of every day together, but as Austin grew into a teenager, he drifted apart from his sister, spending more time in his room alone.

Unfortunately, Austin's sister wasn't the only one who had felt neglected by him. He gradually stopped snuggling with his mom as well, which made her feel sad because she thought she had lost those precious moments with her son. Little did Austin's sister and mother know that he was struggling with his emotions since puberty started. Somehow, he felt different inside, almost as if he was losing who he was before, but he could feel that he was growing into someone else. This phase was terrifying for Austin, and he didn't know how to talk to his family about it. Because Austin's dad had passed away when he was two-years-old, he didn't have that male figure in his life with whom he could share his troubles.

Austin soon fell into depression, and he had to take several pills each day to help him cope with his emotions. His mom felt completely helpless because she didn't know what to do to help her son. As the years went by, Austin engaged in many unhealthy habits, such as smoking and drinking alcohol. When he turned 17, he dropped out of school because he couldn't deal with the pressure. His mental health took a turn for the worst when his mom remarried, and he often remained in his room where he felt safe from the outside world. Austin was crying out for help in the only way he knew how—by isolating himself from his family. Sadly, none of them noticed. Austin's sister and his mother gave up on trying to save Austin from his dark emotions. They continued living their lives, and they stopped checking in on him.

Austin didn't know how to help himself. All he knew was that he wanted to stop feeling so numb and unhappy. The medication he was taking helped him for a while, but deep down he needed love from his family to pull him out of that dark place. Because his mother and sister didn't understand what teenage depression was, they couldn't help Austin. They felt that he was being an attention seeker, so they left him to deal with it on his own. This was the worst decision they ever made because it drove Austin to take his own life in desperation. The reality is, just because you don't understand why a person is depressed, it doesn't mean that they are lying about it or doing it for attention. Austin's family made that mistake, and it cost them his life.

Signs of Mental Health Issues in Teenagers

As mentioned in the first chapter, teenage boys are more prone to becoming depressed mainly because of their fluctuating hormones which cause a chemical imbalance in the brain. While there are also other causes for depression in teenagers, such as constant family conflict, sexual or physical abuse, and poverty, puberty is the most common. Young men struggle with their mental health just as much as girls do, but they aren't as forthcoming about it. Because boys want to come across as being tough, they often choose to hide this sensitive side of themselves out of fear of being judged. However, parents know their children better than anyone else does, so they will be able to notice any signs in their teenager that might indicate they are suffering from a mental health disorder such as depression or anxiety. Here are some of the signs you can look out for in your teenager.

1. Angry outbursts and mood fluctuations.

2. Violent and aggressive behavior toward others, such as getting into fights at school etc.//3. Poor performance at school due to lack of concentration.
4. Lack of interest in the activities they loved participating in before.
5. Withdrawing from their friends and family members.
6. Lethargic and low energy when it comes to any physical activity.
7. Becoming involved with alcohol and drugs.
8. Engaging in risk-taking behavior.
9. A change in their weight.
10. Complaining of headaches and stomach pains.
11. Talking about death, or wanting to harm themselves.

These are some signs to look out for in your teenager that could point towards moderate to severe depression. Although boys are more withdrawn and private about their symptoms, it isn't difficult to recognize these signs if you pay attention. Parents, please don't ignore or overlook the behavior of your teenager. Just because he isn't asking for help with his words doesn't mean he isn't trying to get your attention in other ways. This is how parents make the mistake of brushing things aside, and the next moment they end up burying their children. Remember, your son is a child who is experiencing puberty. He isn't an adult just yet, so he wouldn't understand how to control his emotions. It's still your responsibility as a parent to help your child even when he doesn't think he needs it.

Teenage Depression and Suicide

Suicide is a topic that parents hate talking about, and it doesn't take a scientist to figure out why. The thought of losing a child is more than any parent could bear, so they avoid bringing up this topic with their teenagers. Realistically, your teenager needs to be educated on suicide and mental health, especially when they are already displaying signs of mental health issues. No doubt that it is a tough discussion to have with your child, but think about how it will help him in the long run. Some parents think that talking to their children about suicide will encourage them to take their own lives. This couldn't be more untrue! As a mother or father, it's up to you to ensure that your child is aware of the many ways depression and anxiety can be treated. Suicide is never an option, especially when your teenager isn't of a responsible age to make these decisions. Parents need to be more open and upfront with their teenagers when it comes to talking about mental health and suicide. It's okay if you don't know where to start, or how to approach your teenager with this topic. This chapter is going to provide you with all the guidance you need to save your teenagers life. Once you see things from your teenager's perspective, you will be able to help them get over their thoughts of suicide.

Why Do Teenagers Think About Taking Their Own Lives?

It's vital for parents to learn about what might lead a teenager to take their own lives so that they can prevent any tragedies. Understanding the complex reasons behind why a teenager wants to end their lives, or has attempted to, can be a challenge. Teenagers will be reluctant to open up about their feelings, especially if they feel that their parents don't understand them. Then risks of suicide rise greatly during adolescence, so parents must be vigilant in this regard. According to the CDC, suicide is the third largest cause of death for people aged 15-24 years old. When teens have easy access to firearms, the risk of suicide increases greatly. In the U.S. nearly 60% of suicides (all ages) were committed with a gun. Overdosing is another popular method for teenage suicide since teenagers have easy access to their parents' prescription pills (Cammarata, 2017). Given all the facts above, the big question still stands—why do teenagers think about taking their own lives?

Feeling Discouraged

Teenagers have to deal with many situations in their lives that are often discouraging. Negative situations such as parents losing their jobs or getting a divorce, the death of a loved one, or failing at something that they have been working on for a long time, are all situations that leave a teenager feeling discouraged and dismayed. When these big events take place, teenagers feel like they have no way out because they can't see life getting any better. These are all real-life problems that occur in everyone's lives, but it can be a lot to handle for a teenager who is struggling through puberty. When these major life changes occur, parents need to pay close attention to their children. It's understandable that parents are also facing their own battles, and might not be as attentive to their teenagers. However, it's crucial that you remain hopeful so you can help your teenager through this dark phase in their lives.

Feeling Rejected

Rejection is something we all face in life. Whether it is being rejected by a job application, or being rejected by someone you are interested in romantically, rejection is a part of being human, and we need to learn how to deal with it effectively. Teenagers feel it deeply whenever they are rejected, and it can leave a scar for life. One of the key aspects of being fulfilled as a teenager is finding a place where you belong—a social circle where you fit in. This usually involves experiencing rejection from many other teenagers until you find the right group of people you enjoy being around. Parents also cause rejection to their children when they turn down their ideas and compare them to other teenagers. Wishing your child would be as good as other teenagers causes them to feel rejected by you because they feel like they aren't good enough for you the way they are. While some teenagers manage to get over their issues with rejection, there are others out there who cannot handle the shame. This causes intense emotional pain because they fear that if they aren't good enough to fit in anywhere now, then it's going to be like that in the future as well. It's because of this fear that teenagers contemplate suicide.

Feeling Overwhelmed

Teenagers who are going through puberty often find themselves overcome by several emotions all at once. If you had to take a look inside your teenager's mind, you would see nothing but chaos and confusion. Do you remember what it was like being a teenager? Did you have it all figured out? I guess not! Sometimes, it can be very challenging to calm those raging emotions, especially when you feel like there's no one who can understand what you are going through. Many teenagers end up lashing out at their parents and family members out of frustration, and even becoming involved in fights at school with other teenagers. Emotional dysregulation is a real thing, and it occurs when teenagers cannot regulate their feelings effectively. When faced with a difficult situation, a teenager wouldn't be able to calm himself down, or think clearly to find a way out of the problem. This can be a lot to handle, and it makes them feel like the rest of their lives are going to be the same way. Hence these teenagers contemplate suicide as a way out of living a life they have no control over.

Feeling Defeated

It's true that we all face defeat in our lives, and each of us understands what that feels like. From the time we were children right up until adulthood, there were many situations where we placed all our faith and worked hard only to reap defeat: failing at school, failing in our personal goals we set for ourselves, and even failing our parents and the expectations they had of us. The reality is we can't always win in every area of life, and when we encounter failure, its main purpose is to teach us a lesson and make us stronger. However, teenagers don't understand this. When they constantly encounter failure in every aspect of life that is important to them, they instantly feel as though their lives are over. A teenager's spirit is easily broken, considering they still have that childlike nature in them. When parents don't do enough to encourage their children to try again despite facing failure, it increases their feelings of shame and disappointment in themselves. Defeat takes away a person's will to survive in this harsh world, and many teenagers succumb to their failures and take their own lives.

Treating Depression in Adolescence

Depression in teenagers must be treated as soon as any signs are spotted. Parents should never assume that their teenagers will get over their feelings of depression on their own. Even if your teenager reassures you that they can handle their feelings, and they don't need therapy, it's not safe to believe them and to let things slide. Your teenager will do everything he can to avoid confronting his issues head on. If you allow him to have his way, you are consciously putting your child at risk for developing long-term mental health issues, and even risking his life if he is considering suicide. There are amazing treatments for overcoming and managing depression, and not all of them require your child to be on medication. However, if your teenager has a severe case of depression, medication will be necessary. Parents have a hard time allowing their child to be on any type of depression medication because they fear that their child will become addicted to the medication, or that it will alter their personality in the long run. Don't fear, mom and dad, these medications are usually prescribed for a short period of time to help your child cope with their emotions. There are also other methods of therapy that will help your teenager confront their fears. Here's a list of treatment options available for treating depression in teenagers.

- **Psychotherapy:** This type of treatment involves one on one sessions with a therapist, where your child will be able to talk about their feelings with a professional. Cognitive behavioral therapy is also a good treatment option for mild to moderate cases of depression.

- **Group Therapy**: This therapy treatment is great for teenagers as they talk about their problems as a group. It helps them realize that they aren't the only ones who are struggling with their mental health, and that it is a normal part of life. Group therapy encourages teenagers to form support networks, which is great for helping them overcome depression naturally.

- **Medications**: SSRIs (Serotonin Reuptake Inhibitors) are antidepressant medications given to treat depression in teenagers who are diagnosed with major depressive disorder. In these cases, therapy alone isn't enough to help them overcome their disorder. Teenagers who are at risk for suicide should be evaluated by a doctor before taking any kind of medications.

Strategies Parents Can Use to Bring their Teenagers Out of Depression

During adolescence, teenagers and their parents become distant from one another for several reasons. Most of the time, it's those typical arguments every parent and child has, or it's the moodiness and anger that a teenager feels which makes them want to be alone. Whatever the reason may be, it's important that parents work on rebuilding their relationship with their teenagers. When your teenager has been diagnosed with depression, your role as a parent is vital in their recovery. In their world, the only symbol of safety and security is you–their mother or father. Supporting a child through depression is no easy task. There is a lot you have to put up with, and oftentimes it can be stressful for the parent as well. Maintaining your composure and staying calm is difficult when you are going through the motions; however, it is necessary that you be as supportive as you can for the benefit of your teenager's wellbeing. Below, we take a look at some strategies that you can use to help ease your child out of their depressive state.

Ask Questions to Better Understand What Your Teenager Is Going Through

Gaining an understanding of how your teenager is really feeling is important if you want to help them conquer their battles with their mental health disorders. Consider asking them key questions that will give you an insight into what they are thinking. Both parents shouldn't ask questions at the same time, because it could make your teenager feel uncomfortable. The last thing you want to do is overwhelm your child when they are fragile, or try to make it seem like you are confronting your teenager about something. Choose which parent will talk to your teenager first–preferably the one who is closest to your child. You can ask the following questions:

1. "How are you doing buddy? I'm just wondering why you have been so quiet lately."

2. "Do you mind telling me what's weighing so heavy on your mind?"

3. "Why do you think you are feeling this way?"

4. "Is there something we can do to make you feel better?"

5. "Do you find yourself thinking about death? Or do you sometimes feel like everything would be better if you weren't in this world anymore?"

6. "Do you think that you can handle your emotions, or do they feel out of control?"

7. "Is there a specific reason that has caused you to become depressed?"

Parents, please understand that your child might be reluctant to open up to you at first, especially if their depression has to do with substance abuse or with a romantic relationship. Out of fear of being judged or misunderstood, many teenagers choose to remain quiet about their personal issues. You will have to show your teenager that you come from a place of genuine love and support instead of judging the choices they have made. When talking to your teenager, keep your tone of voice as friendly as you can, because the minute your teenager detects a hint of anger or frustration in your voice, they will immediately withdraw and shut themselves off.

Prepare Yourself to Listen

Once your teenager is ready to start opening up, it's vital that you make time to listen without any distractions. It might take a few tries before your child is able to trust you enough to share what's on their mind, so don't lose hope or give up on them too fast. Depression can sometimes make people think that they are burdening their loved ones, so it takes a lot of mental strength and courage to finally open up to people. When your teenager is ready to talk, try your best to leave whatever it is you are doing and give them your full attention. If you had to answer them with a statement like, "just give me five minutes", or "can we talk about this later?," it will come across as a rejection in the eyes of your child. Bear in mind that your child would pick the right time to talk with you. He wouldn't come to you when he knows you are actively busy with a task; instead, he would wait until he notices that you aren't occupied with anything to approach you. In any case, if you are caught up in a task which cannot be left midway, turn toward your child and explain this to them in the most loving way possible. Make eye contact, hold their hand if you can, and tell your teenager that you will definitely speak with them as soon as you wrap up your work. This will make them feel heard and acknowledged by you. Responding to your child with your back turned will send the message that they aren't important enough for you to stop what you're doing and reply to them. When you are ready to talk, there are a few things you should keep in mind.

- Give your child all of your attention. Put all phones on silent and make it your priority to hear your child.

- Try not to interrupt your teenager while he is talking, even if he takes a bit longer to finish his sentences.

- Pay attention to what *he* is saying to you, trying not to think about what *you* want to say to him.

- Make him feel like you are listening by nodding your head and verbalizing your interest.

- Don't speak for your child, or try to twist his experience to suit your understanding.

- If you don't understand what he is saying, ask for clarification.

- Avoid statements like, "Oh, everyone goes through that," or "It's not such a big deal." These words show that you are not taking your teenager's feelings seriously.

- Instead, use statements like, "I can see how that could make you feel upset," or "I know that you are going through so much, but you are not alone. I'm here to help you."

Give Your Teenager a Break

It's important that your teenager remains involved in household chores and continues to stay active, so encourage them to play sports, to do their chores, and spend time with their friends. However, if your teenager is having a bad day, consider cutting him some slack. Depression is a silent battle we fight inside our heads all the time, and there will be days when we feel like we are losing the battle. If your teenager wants to have a day to lie in bed and not do anything, allow him to do so. After a day or two he will come around to his usual self. If you push him too far, you just might end up causing more harm than good. However, if you notice that his depressive episodes are lasting longer than a few days, take charge and bring him back to reality. Remind your teenager that he has responsibilities he needs to fulfill, and make sure that he is seeing them through. When a break slowly turns into a new way of life, it could be dangerous for those with depression. Allow your son to have his space, but at the same time be ready to reel him back in if you think that he is going too far. There is a fine line between being an overbearing parent and an understanding one. It takes some time to find a balance, but never allow yourself to become one of those parents who want to control everything their child is doing. This behavior will only add on to your teenager's depression and might even send them spiraling downwards. Be patient with your child, trying to understand that they might find it harder to concentrate on tasks, and their energy levels would be low due to their depression. Continue to support them and encourage them to keep their head above water. It's easy to drown in depression when you have no one to snap you out of it, but knowing when to intervene is crucial.

Do Things as a Family

Making changes, as a family, to your lifestyle and routine, is one of the best decisions you can make for your child who is battling with depression. Breaking those old, toxic cycles can make all the difference to some families who have lived in conflict for so long. When a child is depressed, you have to start questioning the environment around you. There are a few questions you can ask yourself to try and figure out why your teenager is so unhappy. It takes a high level of maturity and responsibility for parents to ask themselves these questions, but that's how you know whether you are doing everything you can to help your child.

- "How am I contributing to my child's unhappiness?"
- "Am I spending enough time with my child?"
- "Do I make other aspects of my life a priority over my child?"
- "What can I do to work on myself as a parent?"
- "Is my child growing up in the right environment?"

Sometimes, parents don't realize that they have neglected to think about their child's happiness when they have made certain decisions in their lives. If you feel like you have been lacking as a parent, there are some things you can do about it. Here are a few examples of what parents can do to bring a change into family life.

1. Go on trips together. Consider camping on the beach or going out for picnics with your children.
2. Have supper together at the dining table and put away all devices when you are eating.
3. Spend quality time with one another by engaging in fun activities, such as playing board games, building puzzles, watching movies, or cooking together.
4. Go for a walk after supper and talk about how your day was.
5. Create a healthy routine for the entire family to follow, such as sleeping earlier and waking up earlier.
6. Consider family counseling at least twice a month. This will give each member of the family a chance to voice their concerns in a controlled environment with a qualified professional who can provide guidance on moving forward.

These are examples of the kind of changes you can make to your home as a parent. The foundation of every home should rest on love and respect for one another, regardless of their age. When you make time for your children and start paying attention to what's actually going wrong in your home, you are taking the first steps toward change. It all starts with you, mom and dad! You have to be the ones to spark the change, and the others will eventually follow along. These strategies will make a world of a difference to how you parent your teenager, while also bringing you both closer in the midst of your disagreements.

In Closing

Talking to your teenager about depression and suicide can be a difficult experience. Every parent wants to believe that their child is enjoying their adolescent years by having fun with their friends and doing things that teenagers usually do. However, this isn't always what their experience looks like. Parents don't see when their teenagers are crying in bed, battling with their low self-esteem, or struggling with thoughts about suicide. Your child might be hanging out with their friends, playing sports, and excelling in school, but underneath their mask, they are depressed and angry at their lives. This is why it is important for parents to talk to their children about mental health issues which come up during puberty. Help your child understand that these feelings of depression and anxiety will not last forever. They are temporary, and can be managed effectively with therapy and medications. This chapter has provided you with the information you need to help your child emerge victorious from the depths of depression and other mental health disorders. Remember, communication is vital between parent and child, especially when it comes to mental health concerns.

Chapter 5:
Self Confidence for Teenage Boys

Why It's Important to Love Yourself

This chapter will help parents understand why it's important for boys to have good self-esteem, especially when they are going through puberty. With all of the physical changes taking place in your teenager, it can be a real challenge for them to accept themselves wholeheartedly. That's where you come in, mom and dad. You can help your child build their self-confidence one step at a time, and you can teach them how to love themselves genuinely, without the approval of others.

Teenage Boys and Their Fluctuating Self-Esteem

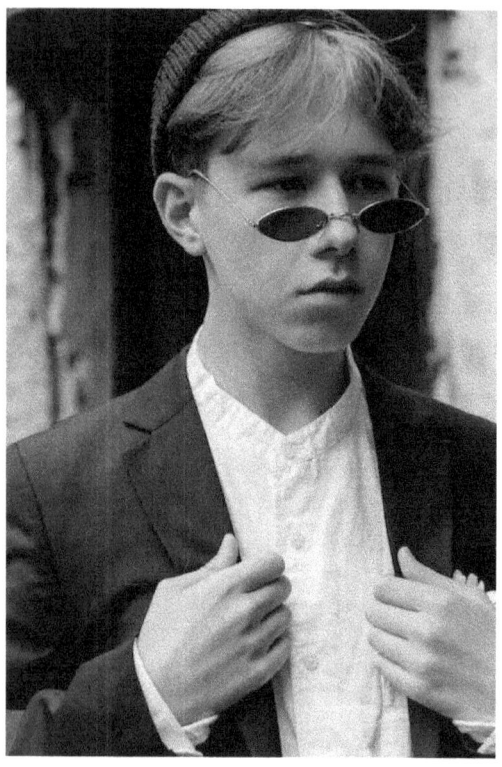

Parents, wouldn't you agree that your teenager's sense of style has completely changed since they hit puberty? They went from dressing in cool shorts and t-shirts to wearing baggy jeans and oversized hoodies which cover their entire body, even in the warmest weather! Have you noticed how your teenager now hates combing his hair, or cleaning his shoes? What could be causing this change in the way they see themselves? Why doesn't your teenager like dressing themselves up smartly? Truth be told, the way your teenager dresses has a lot to do with their self-confidence.

When teenage boys hit puberty, they begin to notice changes taking place in their body. Sometimes, these changes can be uncomfortable because they alter the boy's physical appearance so much that he no longer recognizes himself. Growth spurts are a common part of adolescence, and when they occur, teenagers often find themselves feeling insecure about certain parts of their body.

Joshua's Experience

Joshua had just turned 14 when he woke up one morning in utter disbelief over what he saw in the mirror. Joshua wasn't mentally prepared for the physical developments that were taking place with his body. He noticed hair growing on his chin, and a faint, but recognizable, mustache on his face, which made him feel a bit uncomfortable. In Joshua's mind, he was still very much a child, and the last thing he wanted was to start looking like a grown man! Apart from the facial hair, Joshua's body odor hadn't been all that tolerable lately. He became very self-conscious about the way he smelled whenever he was around other people. Joshua tried all sorts of deodorants and body sprays, but none of them were effective enough to eliminate the smell. Joshua lived in South America, a place with one of the hottest climates ever. All the sweating made his body odor issues worse, so Joshua eventually lost confidence in himself. Because he was raised by a single mom, Joshua didn't know how to shave. His facial hair continued to grow, and other boys at school always made fun of him because he was the only boy in his class who grew a mustache.

There was this one time Joshua's classmates bullied him into shaving his facial hair. They had brought a shaver to school and forced Joshua to shave off his mustache. This bullying incident completely destroyed all of Joshua's self-confidence. He didn't want to go to school anymore, and he often made excuses of being ill just so he could stay home. He refused to tell his mother what happened at school. Instead, he kept it all inside– bottled up tightly. Without the support or empathy from his mother, Joshua fell into deep depression. He no longer felt good enough about himself, and whenever he saw his facial hair growing back, he would instantly shave it off. Consequently, Joshua missed out on enjoying his teenage years. He carried his insecurities with him into adulthood. Even though he finally managed to control his body odor and keep his facial hair neat, he always felt insecure within himself.

Joshua found himself expressing his insecurities on social media anonymously. He was surprised to see that there were so many people who went through the same experience during their years of puberty. Pouring his heart out to others helped him get over his issues with low self-esteem, and their support helped him build up his confidence again. Because Joshua never opened up to his mother during his teen years, or spoke about his issues with his friends, he had no idea that he wasn't the only one feeling uncomfortable and ashamed of his body. If only he had reached out to someone for help, he would have realized that every teenager, both boys and girls, have insecurities about themselves. Unfortunately, he had to learn this after many years of suffering in silence.

The Importance of Self-Confidence in Teenage Boys

In today's modern world, teenagers are being bombarded left and right with adverts and videos that are aimed at improving their physical appearance. Suddenly, the world now perceives a teenager's developing body as something that is unnatural and not acceptable. There are adverts for products that promise to get rid of teenage acne, weight gain, facial and body hair, and other "imperfections" which teenagers have to endure during puberty. When did it become okay to target teenagers and make them feel like they aren't perfect the way they are? Parents, do you remember what the so-called "beauty standards" were back when you were a teenager? Children who were experiencing puberty were allowed to be themselves. There was no judgment or backlash for having a certain body type because people weren't as shallow back then as they are now. Boys also have a hard time with their self-esteem, yet the focus is always placed on teenage girls and their issues with body image and self-confidence. Having good self-esteem is just as important for teenage boys, as it is for girls. There are several benefits that come with having positive self-esteem. Below, we take a look at a few of these incredible benefits.

Healthy Interpersonal Relationships

Building relationships with other teenagers is a vital part of being a teenager, and the only way your child can do this is if they are confident in themselves. Have you ever seen a timid or shy teen willingly approach a group of boys and try to strike up a conversation with them? The reason why this rarely ever happens is because the shy teenager has no confidence in himself. When you have a healthy self-esteem, and you are secure in who you are, it will be easy to make new friends and adjust to social settings quicker than others. Because of your confidence, you are able to mix well with other teenagers, and you get to experience the joy of friendship on a different level. Whether it's at school, work, or soccer practice, people will be drawn to you, and you can have a great relationship with others.

Being Open to Trying New Things

Confidence gives you the ability to be open and accepting when it comes to trying new things in life. You will have no apprehension or fear of the unknown because you are well-settled within yourself. If someone had to come up to you and ask you to perform a dance in front of others, you would be able to accept their request because of how much confidence you have in yourself. You don't care about being embarrassed or falling flat on your face, as long as you are having fun. When you have low self-esteem, you wouldn't jump at the opportunity to try new things. There is a fear of being embarrassed or failing at this new task because you don't believe that you have what it takes to be successful in it. This fear is what holds teenagers back from truly experiencing life, and they miss out on so much because of their insecurities.

Better Performance in School and in Other Activities

Teenagers who are confident in themselves often excel in their school work, as well as in the extra-curricular activities they participate in. The motivation to give their all and be the very best must come from within. Remember that the mind is a place of chaos, especially when you have been fighting an invisible battle against your low self-esteem. How can there be any motivation or encouragement to keep pushing to keep your grades up if your mind is insecure? Only a confident mind will be able to work through all the distractions and remain positive that they can complete the task at hand by giving their very best. This is essential if you want to succeed in life as an adult. It all starts now during the teenage years. Knowing what you are capable of and harnessing your full potential is only possible through being confident and secure about yourself.

Finding Happiness Easily and Being More Content With Life

Close your eyes for a minute, and picture two teenage boys—one very insecure, and the other quite confident and sure of who he is. How are the looks on their faces different? My guess would be that the former looks sad and defeated, while the latter has a big bright smile on his face. Isn't it obvious which one is more content with their lives? It's much easier to find happiness when you are confident because you tend to enjoy the little things in life. You don't need to spend lots of money on expensive gadgets to find happiness because your joy comes from within yourself. When a person is insecure, they try to fulfill themselves with material goods such as designer clothing, expensive phones, and fancy jewelry. But these things only bring temporary satisfaction. Until you are confident in who you are, happiness will be hard to find.

Persevering Through Trials

When life hits, it hits very hard. Most people are not strong enough to face the battles in their lives because they lack self-confidence. They truly believe in their heart of hearts that they cannot face these trials because they don't have what it takes. Teenagers have to learn the importance of staying strong throughout life's storms. They can only persevere if they have faith in themselves. If you don't trust yourself enough, you will never make it out of your negative situation. A positive self-confidence keeps you hopeful and strong in the face of adversity. No matter what you encounter in your life, you will emerge more than a conqueror because you believe in yourself. That is why it is important to have good self-esteem, especially during adolescence—one of the most challenging phases of life.

Parents, it's crucial that you teach your children the importance of having positive self-confidence as a teenager. This is the time when your teenager learns critical life skills which they will use later on in adulthood. Speak to your child about the benefits of being a confident individual, as mentioned above, and help them understand how this can impact their lives in the long run. While it's important that you acknowledge the reasons why your child has lost his self-esteem, you shouldn't dwell too much on the problem. Instead, spend time working on helping your child build their confidence so they can face all their hardships in life without giving up. You might think that your teenager is too immature to understand how important his self-confidence is, and because of this assumption, you might not want to talk to him about it. However, this is a mistake many parents make with their children. Don't be afraid to educate your child on these important aspects of life because the world has changed, and they need guidance in every department of life, irrespective of their age.

Overcoming Shame as a Teenage Boy

Shame plays a huge role in teenage depression and self-esteem issues, and parents shouldn't allow their teenagers to carry guilt and shame for prolonged periods of time. Yes, if your teenager does something they know they shouldn't have, it is important for them to understand the consequences of their actions. Often this involves allowing them to feel ashamed of the choices they have made, hoping that they will learn from their mistakes. However, there is a good chance that your teenager might become overwhelmed by their feelings of guilt and shame. When this happens, it can lead to long-term problems with their self-esteem and their mental health. Teenage boys are famous for acting without thinking as well as for doing stupid things that they will regret later on. It's a part of the learning and evolution of a teenager. A teenage boy wouldn't think twice about engaging in risky behavior in which he could end up hurting himself, or someone else in the process. As long as he learns from his mistakes and makes better decisions moving forward, he shouldn't have to carry around debilitating guilt or shame that takes over his life. That is why it's imperative that parents help their children come out of their guilt and shame so that they can live their lives to the fullest, given that they understand what shame is and why they feel it.

What Is Shame?

Shame can be described as a painful feeling of embarrassment or humiliation which sets in after a person has done something foolish. For example, you gossip with your friends at work about the new employee who is still learning the ropes, yet you know that it is wrong to talk about people behind their back. So when this new employee finds out you have been talking smack about them, and they confront you about it, you instantly feel ashamed of your actions. Eventually, guilt sets in when you think about what you have done to hurt another person's reputation.

Everyone does things in their lives that they regret, and we all wish we could go back in time to right our wrongs. The reason why we feel remorse for our actions is because we are driven by shame and guilt. These emotions serve a purpose in our lives, and that is to prick our conscience whenever we do something that goes against our beliefs. However, shame and guilt can be damaging when they take over an individual's entire life.

The Impact of Shame and Guilt

Long term feelings of shame and guilt can have a negative impact on a teenager's life. It's crucial therefore that parents and their teenagers recognize the signs of destructive guilt and shame the moment it sets in. These feelings will be so intense that your teenager might feel like they cannot function normally. Here are some of the signs you can look out for.

- Oversleeping to avoid thinking about the situation.
- Performing poorly at school, which causes their grades to drop drastically.
- Losing interest in doing things they previously enjoyed.
- Avoiding their friends and family because they are ashamed.
- Losing or gaining weight due to changes in their appetite.
- Failing to appreciate a compliment because they feel unworthy.

When a person feels intense shame and guilt, they are instinctively motivated to do something to correct their actions and to make things right. They become obsessed with the idea of repenting for their mistakes and gaining the forgiveness of the person they hurt. The remorse can greatly impact the day-to-day life of that person, and without proper emotional regulation, they begin to lose themselves. Now, can you imagine how life would be for a teenager who is carrying around guilt and shame for a mistake they have made? If parents don't intervene in time to get their teenager some help, they could end up falling into severe depression in a matter of days, which might then lead to suicide.

Potential Situations That Could Leave a Teenager Feeling Ashamed

Teenagers are very naive, and because of their inexperience, they are prone to making mistakes. These mistakes could have a deep impact on the conscience of your teen, especially if you have instilled certain values and morals in them from a young age. Since parents were once teenagers, they are aware of the fact that there are several different situations that might catch you off guard. The choices you make in those situations are what matters. But because teenagers are young and fresh out of childhood, they don't have the ability to make wise decisions yet. This is what causes feelings of shame and guilt to crop up later on. Let's take a look at some of the mistakes managers commonly make during adolescence, which they later regret.

- Experimenting with drugs and alcohol, which eventually becomes a habit.
- Skipping out on school and getting bad grades as a result.
- Engaging in sexual activity with the wrong people.
- Making a girl pregnant or developing an STD because of unprotected sex.
- Getting involved in fights with other teenagers, and being violent.
- Following the crowd and behaving the same way your friends do.
- Sending nude pictures of oneself on social media chat sites.

- Being publicly humiliated by a bully.

The above-mentioned experiences are quite common for teenagers, and there is no way you can avoid any of them. Sooner or later, your teenager is going to experience a situation like this where they feel ashamed. It's understandable that your child might not have the life skills he needs to overcome these situations within a reasonable amount of time, as he is still young and lacks the experience. However, parents can use this opportunity to teach their teenagers the importance of facing their guilt and shame before it completely takes over their lives.

Ways Parents Can Help their Teenagers Face their Shame and Overcome the Strongholds of Guilt

Most adults struggle with defeating their shame and controlling their guilt. Even at their mature age, they cannot fathom how destructive intense feelings of shame and guilt can be. The truth is that we are still learning and growing each day, and with every experience we go through, there are valuable lessons which we must take away with us. Parents, the lessons which you have learned in your life so far can be extremely beneficial for your teenager. You can help your child get over their shame by teaching them key strategies that will enable them to face their feelings and learn from their mistakes without punishing themselves continuously. Below, you will find some amazing tips that you can utilize in your attempts to help your teenager heal and find their confidence again.

Don't Be Judgmental or Critical

The shame monster often whispers words of discouragement into your child's ears. One of the key goals of this shame monster is to make your teenager believe that his parents are going to think that he is unworthy of love because of the mistake he made. It successfully gets your teenager to believe that they won't be loved or accepted by their parents, or by their friends any longer. This could be the first time your child is experiencing these feelings, and he wouldn't know how to quiet the voices inside his head which are telling him how unworthy he is. Parents, this is where you can help your teenager change the direction of his thinking before it forms into a habit that lasts a lifetime. Yes, as a parent you will be hurt that your child has done something that went against his values. But being judgmental or critical about it is only going to make things worse. If you point fingers at your child, or always remind him of the mistake he made, he is going to internalize that and do it to himself as well. It takes a mature parent to understand that their children are going to mess up at times and do things that could end up costing them their future. We have all made mistakes when we were younger, so it's only normal that we would want our kids to make the right choices in their lives. However, it's still their choice at the end of the day. And we as parents should guide them and support them, not judge them.

Accept and Validate Your Teenager's Experience

Parents tend to forget that their teenagers are going through this phase in their lives for the very first time. They are still discovering who they are, and this often involves making a lot of wrong decisions in the process. The reason why teenagers barely open up to their parents about their lives is that they feel that their mothers and fathers won't understand their experience. When you make your child feel indifferent because of the choices he made, it can greatly impact his self-confidence. Just because you didn't share the same experience as your child when you were a teenager, it doesn't mean that your child's experience is out of the ordinary. The world has changed a lot since you were a teen, so it's obvious that your experiences won't be exactly the same. The best way to understand why your child has done something is by putting yourself in their shoes. Try to see things from their perspective and offer validation to show that you can relate. By validating your child's experience, you are showing them that you understand what they are going through. This breaks down the walls your teenager has built as a defense mechanism and improves the communication between parent and child. Now, you can advise and help your child without them shutting you out.

Help Them Rebuild Their Self-Confidence

Shame has the ability to completely annihilate a person's confidence and trust in themselves. When this happens, it becomes very difficult to break out of that toxic mindset which your teenager has created for himself. As long as your teenager believes that he is shameful and unworthy, he will never be able to find the confidence he needs to move forward. That is why it is so important for parents to think about everything they say or do to their teenager, because their words and actions could either further break their child's confidence or give them the boost they need to get over their shame. Moms and dads, your child depends on you for so much! Even though they try to show you that they are independent and capable of making their own decisions, at the end of the day, they turn to you in times of trouble. The best thing you can do during this time is try to encourage and motivate your teenager. Reassure them that they can learn from their mistakes and make wiser decisions in the future. When they open up and talk to you about their mistakes, don't make it seem like it's the end of the world, but also help them understand the gravity of the situation. Boost their confidence by reminding them of how intelligent and talented they are, and push them to stay committed to their hobbies in spite of their mistakes.

In Closing

As adults, we understand the importance of having a healthy self-esteem, especially when it comes to interacting with people, going for job interviews, and even dating. When you have no confidence in yourself, you cannot achieve your goals or expect people to take you seriously.

Hence, parents should always motivate and cheer their children on, no matter what situations they have to face in life. If you, as a parent, can discipline your child for their mistakes, but also encourage them to love themselves and not give up on their dreams, then you will definitely succeed in raising responsible, confident human beings. It is possible to be strict, and to hold your kids accountable for their actions without bringing them down or making them feel worse about the mistakes they have made. Be wise parents and think maturely. Your child's future is in your hands, so how you choose to handle the difficult situations now, will determine the character your child develops in the future.

Chapter 6:
School Might Suck, But You Need It!

The Importance of Being Educated and Having Goals

In this short, yet informative, chapter, you will learn how to talk to your son about the importance of going to school and getting good grades. There are key sections highlighted in this chapter which will help you see things from your teenager's perspective. Once you develop an understanding of why your child hates school, you will know what to say to them, and how to say it, so that they become motivated and excited to pursue their education. When you give up on your children, they give up on themselves too. So please push your teenager to have goals for their lives, because life isn't exciting without them. We all need to work towards something for the betterment of our future, or else what are we going to do with ourselves?

Why Do Education and Goal-Setting Matter?

Mention the word "homework" to any teenager, and watch as their face quickly turns sour! Oh, how they hate that dreaded "H" word, and anyone who mentions it to them (parents and teachers) becomes their arch enemy. Okay, I'm sure we can agree that homework wasn't our go to activity when we were younger. Even if you were the most intelligent child in the whole class, you probably hated doing homework as well. What about having to wake up early on those cold winter mornings to go to school, even though you want to sleep in because you are warm under the covers. If we hated all these things about school, why would we expect our children to love them instead? Yes, education is very important, and as parents we should always rally behind our kids, pushing them to stay committed to their education. However, we shouldn't ignore our reality in the process. We need to use a different approach when trying to talk to our children about education, because nagging them sure ain't helping. Let's start off by explaining why education is so important these days.

Top Five Reasons Why Education is Important

Education has been one of the top priorities in many developing countries, such as India, South Africa, and Brazil. This is because these countries understand how education can help boost their economy by producing competent people who can make sound and informed decisions about their lives and their communities. Education can change your life for the better because it opens your eyes to how the world really works. Parents can help their teenagers understand the importance of education by elaborating on the benefits mentioned below.

#1 Education Provides Stability and Financial Security

Every human being wants to be stable in life, without worrying about where their next meal is coming from. Financial security is one of the most important goals you could ever set for your life because it determines how your future would be like. If you have a good education, you stand a better chance of finding a well-paying job that provides you with that financial security you need. Even if you don't see yourself working for someone else, you can still start your own business with the knowledge and experience you have gained through your education.

#2 Education is Crucial For Equality

The truth is, in this day and age if you want to live a life that is equal to others, you have to be educated to do so. There are millions of people who lack an education, which is why they are forced to live in different areas, shop at different stores, and work in different jobs. There is a clear division which exists between those who have been educated and those who are not, and unfortunately, the only way you can ever be considered equal is if you have an education behind you to help you succeed in life. For example, a woman who has been educated can perform the job of a man because she now has been trained and skilled to do so. However, if she lacks the proper credentials, she might never be considered for the job. That's just how the world works these days.

#3 Education Makes You Feel More Confident in Yourself

In general, people are more confident in themselves when they understand what is going on in the world around them. Being educated gives you the opportunity to stand up for yourself when you disagree with something because you feel more confident that you are making the right decision. Without a proper education, you will often question yourself about whether you are making the right decision or not. When you have an education, you can freely participate in any event or activity without stressing that you will embarrass yourself, because you can adapt to any situation–all thanks to your education.

#4 Education Can Help You Reach Your Goals

Goals and dreams often need a reliable vehicle to get to the place where they can become a reality. Everyone has a vision in their minds of what they want their lives to be like, and we can spend hours daydreaming about these goals because it makes us happy. However, what use are dreams if we cannot turn them into a reality? Without a good education, it becomes almost impossible to make your dreams come true. Teenagers fail to recognize that education gives them the power they need to achieve their goals, no matter how big or small they are. Whether you dream of flying an airplane or owning a business, both dreams require you to study and gain a qualification.

#5 Education Protects You

A lot of people fall prey to scams these days because they don't have the knowledge or understanding when it comes to certain aspects of life. Consider the Bitcoin scam which robbed people of millions in Bitcoin (digital currency). Most people who invested in this scam had no prior knowledge about that field, and this proved to be a massive downfall for them. It's easier to fool an uneducated person because they know nothing about the world. Your education doubles up as a shield which protects you from becoming a target for people to take advantage of you. The more you know about the world, the better your chances of identifying potential threats.

The Benefits of Goal-Setting

Setting goals is the first step in turning the invisible into the visible. –Tony Robbins

Goals are an essential part of life. Without them, we would have no sense of direction or purpose, nor would we be motivated to keep moving forward in the midst of our trials. Teenagers don't understand what it means to have a dream for the future, a vision of where you picture yourself ten years from now. They live for the day, and they don't think much about the future. Goals come in two main categories, short term and long term. Short term goals are generally focused on achieving something within five years or less, while long term goals involve a time frame of about six years or more. It's important for teenagers to learn how to set clear goals for themselves. It will teach them how to become responsible by making them commit to something that can only be made possible through their own hard work. Parents should always encourage their teenagers to pursue their goals and to work hard in pursuit of their dreams. Let's take a look at some of the benefits of having goals.

- Providing direction to teenagers: When you set goals for yourself, you are giving yourself something to work towards. This is great for teenagers because it teaches them how to aim for something and then put in the hard work to achieve that dream. Goals provide direction in life, and when a youngster has direction, he won't fall into trouble easily.

- Fostering critical decision-making skills: When it comes to working towards your goals, people often have to face difficult decisions in the process. This is great for helping a teenager develop good decision-making skills early on in life.

- Giving you the power to decide your future: The only way you can ever try to control your future is by planning for it. Goal setting forms a major part of the planning process, and it makes the journey completely yours. When your teenager sets a goal for himself, he is unknowingly taking control of his future.

- Keeping you motivated: Your goals keep you motivated to keep pushing during the difficult moments in life. When your teenager doesn't feel like going to school, his goals can help him realize that life can be better in the future, if only he works hard now.

- Helping you succeed and grow: The road to achieving your goals is a long, tiring one. A lot of people usually give up in the middle of their journey because they do not have the willpower to carry on. But for those people who stick to their goals, and achieve success, they become better versions of themselves because of the lessons they have learned.

How Goal-Setting and Education Work Hand in Hand

As mentioned earlier, if you want to achieve your goals you need to have a good education to empower yourself to do so. Goal setting can help your teenager get through their schooling years without hating school so much. Because parents make school seem like a chore, many teenagers refuse to give their 100% to it. They feel that they would much rather spend their time and energy on something else. If this sounds like your teenager, then this section could help you. The key lies with getting your teenager to enjoy school, and the only way they can do this is by setting small goals which are easy to accomplish, thus bringing happiness and fulfillment to your child. Set goals for achieving a certain percentage in each subject, or to spend a certain amount of time studying every week. These little goals will help your teenager understand how the process works, and the little rewards will motivate him to strive for even bigger goals.

Once goal setting becomes a habit, your teenager won't hesitate to challenge himself to go after the dreams that might seem difficult. Armed with the right knowledge and education, your teenager will be able fulfill any dream he sets his mind on. Education can help you work smarter towards your goals. Instead of following old fashioned, outdated methods which yield no results, you can create your own method of achieving your goals which works best for you. Help your teenager understand how this process works so they become motivated to follow their dreams.

In Closing

The importance of education cannot go ignored. That is why you find there are certain teenagers who take their education seriously, and some who don't. It all has to do with how much their parents encourage them to stay committed to their education. The best way you can convince your teenager to stay in school is by explaining how they will benefit from it in the long run. When it comes to youngsters today, they have to get something to give something. They will only budge when they see how they can benefit from working hard in school. This chapter has given you the information you need to tactfully explain to your teenager what they stand to gain from schooling. Don't nag them about it, and instead talk to them like you would an adult. Keep the conversation short and to the point—just like this chapter!

Chapter 7:
Addressing Addictive Behaviors

Alcohol, Smoking, Drugs... and Even Gaming!

This chapter aims to help parents confront their teenagers' addictive behaviors. There is a certain manner in which parents should approach this conversation with their teenagers that won't scare them away. The fear of losing their children to these addictions often overpowers a parent's willingness to discipline their child because they are afraid of causing more harm than good. This chapter will teach you how to take charge and be the responsible parent your teenager needs.

Addictive Behaviors in Teenage Boys

Teenage boys are more prone to developing addictive behaviors in adolescence than girls are. This makes it difficult to get inside their minds, to find out more about the way they think. There is a shared belief that teenage boys are more outgoing and open when it comes to engaging in risky behaviors, especially when their friends are influencing them negatively. Parents might think that just because their teenager knows about the dangers of substances, they won't get involved with it. This is a dangerous way of thinking because teenagers base their decisions on what they see instead of what they hear. You could tell your child that smoking is wrong and harmful for their health, but if they see you doing it, they aren't going to think that smoking is all that bad. Unfortunately, the world has become so corrupt that smoking and drinking alcohol are portrayed as the "cool" thing to do. Teenagers can become addicted to various things quickly, within a short period of time, so parents should never underestimate their children.

Top Five Addictive Behaviors of Teenagers

There are several things teenagers can become addicted to, and they often develop addictions to more than one of these things. Most parents don't realize that their children have the capability, and understanding, to engage in these activities which are not good for their health or their wellbeing. Below, we take a look at the different things teenagers become addicted to during their adolescent years. This might be shocking to some parents, but the truth is never easy to face.

Alcohol

Who doesn't enjoy a nice glass of wine or a chilled beer every now and then, just to relax and take the edge off? Alcohol can paradoxically calm you down and make you feel excited at the same time. This feeling of euphoria is extremely addictive, which is why so many people become alcoholics. The horrific reality is that there are teenagers who are also addicted to alcohol, not just adults! Because puberty can be such a stressful time in a teen's life, they often look for outlets to expel some of their frustrations. Alcohol becomes the perfect tool to help them escape from their reality. Teenagers are very naive, so they fall into addiction very fast. If something makes them feel good and takes away their bad emotions, they will dive head first into it. This is why so many teenage boys have become addicted to drinking alcohol regularly.

Smoking

Smoking is probably the most common substance teenagers become addicted to during adolescence. It starts off as a casual act, which many teenage boys engage in to "look cool" in school, and before you know it, they can't go a day without smoking. This habit develops into a dangerous addiction that follows teenagers into adulthood. While there is no intense feeling of euphoria when you smoke, it does help to relieve stress and calm you down when you are nervous. However, this isn't enough to make people addicted. It's the nicotine that is found inside the cigarettes which creates the addiction, and teenagers are not wise enough to understand this, so they become addicted fast.

Drugs

The world of drug addiction is a sad one, and all parents are extremely scared of their children falling into this type of addiction. Once a teenager becomes involved with these high-risk drugs, the chances of them losing their lives triples overnight. Drugs such as heroin, crystal meth, ecstasy, and cocaine are widely available at schools and at parties where teenagers hang out. All it takes is one time to become addicted. Even if your teenager hasn't taken it themselves, there is still a risk of someone spiking his drink. A teenager will slowly lose himself in his drug addiction, and the majority of the time, their parents don't even realize it.

Sex

Believe it or not, but teenagers are at high risk of becoming addicted to sex because of their inability to control their urges, which are incredibly high during puberty. When a teenage boy is exposed to pornography, it doesn't take long for his desire to become sexually active awakens. Without the right knowledge and guidance, his sexual behavior can get out of hand quickly. Sexual addiction is just as dangerous as drug addiction and alcohol addiction because the consequences can have detrimental impacts on your life. Unwanted teenage pregnancy, sexually transmitted diseases, and having numerous sexual partners are all negative impacts of being sexually irresponsible.

Gaming

Gaming has trumped many of the other addictions, especially since the Covid-19 pandemic that started in 2020. Teenagers were forced to remain in their homes for months, without being able to participate in their hobbies or seeing their friends. All they had for entertainment was a cellphone and television to pass their time. Many teenagers spent their time gaming on their smart devices, and others chose to use their gaming consoles. Whenever they sat down to play these games, they couldn't even realize how minutes turned into hours, and how hours turned into days. Although everything seems to have gone back to normal, many teenagers continue to be addicted to their gaming. Teenage boys can forget about school, about their family, and even about their food the minute they sit down with their games. Gaming addiction has contributed to eyesight problems, brain problems, and behavioral problems in many teenagers, and it has also affected their ability to socialize in the real world.

Why Are Teenage Addictions So Prevalent Today?

Parents, the only way you are ever going to help your child is if you first develop an understanding of why they are prone to falling into addictive behavior these days. Being a teenager in today's world is very different from being a teenager in the late 90's and early 2000's. Technology has opened the doors for teenagers to become influenced easily, and it all happens without them having to leave their rooms. Here are a few reasons why teenagers fall into addiction so easily.

Social Media

The world of social media has blown up astonishingly over the past few years, starting with MySpace, Facebook, and Instagram, leading up to the current sensation–TikTok! There's no denying that social media has changed the world for the better, in ways that we didn't think was ever possible. However, it has also negatively impacted its users, causing emotional distress, temptation, and embarrassment. Teenagers spend endless hours on social media, and it's almost like they are physically present here, but mentally living inside their phones. This addiction makes it easier for them to become influenced by others, to do things that go against their values. Social media influencers are talented individuals who have a way of glorifying drugs, alcohol, and sex–making it look normal and acceptable for people of all ages. Teenagers are on social media, posting about their sex lives, and their Saturday night partying habits, and they are gaining millions of likes and views from other teenagers. This promotes unacceptable behavior and normalizes addictions, which is the perfect recipe for influencing teenagers.

Music

Music has changed drastically over the past couple of years. If you had to casually turn on the radio, you would only hear songs about money, sex, drugs, and alcohol. Every rap song highlights the use of substances, and the desire to chase after money. Every so-called "love" song focuses a lot on sex rather than on the meaning of true love. Your teenager is listening to these kinds of music daily, and it is slowly brainwashing them into believing that addictions are the new way of life. Parents will understand the message that is being sent through these songs, but teenagers won't be able to because they are now familiar with these kinds of music. The singers and rappers who make vulgar and obscene music are seen as role models to teenagers and even some children. They earn millions of dollars by selling their songs, and then they showcase their fancy lives on social media. This is how youngsters are misled into believing that alcohol and drugs will guarantee you a good life.

A Rise in Mental Health Issues

There has been a rapid growth in the number of teenagers who develop depression and other mental health issues during puberty. Nowadays, young people don't have the ability to withstand any type of emotional disturbances in their lives. They have been weakened by technology and social media, so much so that they cannot handle the stress from little situations. This rapid increase of mental health issues has caused many teenagers to seek comfort in other things. Using alcohol and drugs, being sexually active, and getting lost in the world of gaming–they all provide a sort of escapism for these youngsters. The pleasure they gain from these unhealthy behaviors lasts only a little while, but it's enough to make them think that they feel "normal" when they are under the influence of alcohol or drugs. The absence of emotional pain doesn't mean that you are normal. We all have to face what comes our way no matter how hard life gets, and when teenagers use addictive behaviors to help them cope with mental health issues, it turns into a lifelong issue that destroys their peace.

Easy Access to Sex and Substances

Teenagers never had easy access to alcohol, drugs, and sex back in the day. If a teenage boy wanted to find out more about sex, he would have had to steal a nude magazine from the gas station. If he wanted to experiment with alcohol or drugs, he would steal them from his father (which was a mission). These things weren't so easily available prior to the year 2000. After that, the world started changing drastically, and teenagers had more access to these substances. Now, there are different types of drugs being sold at school, around the block, and even at places of worship, and the most shocking part is that these things are being sold by teenagers! Young girls are becoming involved in prostitution, and they are doing this while at school with other teenage boys. Parents, your children aren't safe from these addictions. They pop up everywhere you turn, and the only way your teenager can avoid them is if they understand how these addictions will ruin their lives.

Understanding the Seriousness of Gaming Addiction

Gaming addiction rates have been growing steadily among teenagers. Teenage boys spend an average of two hours a day playing either video games, or games on their smartphones and tablets. They can spend up to four hours or more on gaming during the weekend because they don't have to attend school on those days. What was intended to bring entertainment and fun has transformed into a dangerous addiction which takes over a teenager's life without them noticing it. Parents might think that video gaming is harmless, and many of them encourage their teenagers to play by buying them gaming consoles and computers. They think that it's better if their children are at home playing games, instead of out there on the street, where there is crime and addictions. However, these parents haven't been made aware of the dangers of video gaming for prolonged periods of time. In this section, you will learn about the impact of gaming addiction, and how it can negatively impact your teenager.

The Dangers of Gaming Addiction

As the famous saying goes, too much of a good thing is bad for you. When it comes to the little pleasures of life, such as eating junk foods, or binge-watching TV series, people tend to go overboard and lose control of themselves. We understand that life can be very hard sometimes, especially when you have many responsibilities to take care of, so it's good that people indulge in the things that make them feel happy and distracted from the real world. After all, it's these little joys and distractions that keep us going. The problem starts when these distractions quickly turn into addictions. Teenagers turn to gaming as a way of escaping their realities. Some teenagers who are bullied in real life rely on video games to help them gain back their lost confidence. Others play video games to escape their turbulent home environment. Whatever the reason, teenage boys are drawn to the world of gaming, and they often fall into addiction fast. Here's why gaming addiction can be dangerous for your child.

Loss of Interest in Other Activities

When a teenager becomes addicted to gaming, they instantly lose interest in the healthy activities they were involved in before. Soccer, chess, dance classes, and math clubs–all take a back seat in your teenager's life because they have replaced all those activities with one unhealthy addiction: video gaming. Without these extra-curricular activities, our teenagers won't be able to develop any social skills, or critical thinking skills.

Moodiness and Aggressive Behavior

Video gaming is all about immersing yourself into the experience, and playing as if your life depended on it. When teenagers play these violent games which involve vulgar language, killing, fighting, weapons, and firearms, they begin to develop a shift in their personality because of the violence in the game. Parents will notice a change in their child's behavior. They will snap at you for little reasons, develop an attitude, and become moody all the time, especially when you restrict their access to gaming. Aggressive behavior should not be overlooked or tolerated by parents, so when you notice that your child has taken a turn for the worst, take action fast.

Poor Grades

The more time a teenager spends on video gaming, the less time he will have to focus on his school work. During exams, he will make every excuse not to study, and even if he does, his mind will be entirely consumed by the video game. Soon, his grades will drop, and he won't be able to catch up with the rest of his class. This will impact his confidence, and make him feel like he is incompetent in his school work. A teenager who doesn't have control over his gaming addiction sets himself up for failure in every aspect of his future career.

Loss of Touch With Reality

As with all addictions, once you are too far gone, you begin to lose touch with reality. The same applies to gaming addiction. Teenagers who are addicted to video gaming, gradually lose touch with the world around them. They have no sense of time, they aren't aware of what's happening in their homes, their connections with their families begin to drift away, and in extreme cases, they even forget to eat and take a shower! I don't have to tell you how disturbing that really is, especially for a young person who has his entire life in front of him. These teenagers who allow their addiction to get so far, lose their desire to live in the real world. To them, there is nothing that is more exciting or rewarding than living in their virtual reality of gaming.

How Parents Can Help Their Children Break Their Addictive Behaviors

Breaking addictive behaviors is no walk in the park. Parents have to be emotionally and mentally strong to help their children, especially when they are out of control. Their stubbornness and aggression gets in the way, and many parents cannot handle this so they choose to let things be. When a parent gives up on their child, it's almost as if they are walking away from them, leaving their children to deal with their issues on their own. If you are a parent who wants to help your teenager break their addiction to gaming, sex, drugs, or alcohol, carry on reading because there are some amazing tips highlighted below that can help you on our journey.

Stop Criticizing and Start Motivating

Parents, the last thing your teenager wants to hear is you telling them just how useless they have become because of their addiction. Sometimes, telling your teenager what they want to hear is the right thing to do. Consider it from this perspective, your teenager has already developed addictive behavior, and nothing you say or do will turn back time. Now, your focus should be on how you can change the future. Your teenager is lost in his addiction, and he isn't feeling good about it either. There's no way that he is happy and thriving in his addiction, so you need to become the lifeline he needs to pull himself out of that darkness. Speak words of encouragement to him and keep reminding him of how talented and intelligent he is. Mention all the good things you love about your child, because he needs to hear it so he can find himself again.

Introduce New Activities For Him to Try

When teenagers become involved with addiction, they tend to forget about the things they loved doing before. They lose interest in their hobbies, and sometimes they refuse to take them on again out of fear of not being good enough. Parents can help their children discover new hobbies and talents by encouraging them to try new things. Every teenager has their own likes and dislikes, and they often become set on doing things that they like. This can make it harder for parents to get their children to try new stuff, so think of activities that match your teenager's personality. Once they start opening themselves up to trying new things, you can get them involved in other fun activities. When your teenager finds something new to spend their time doing, they will eventually lose interest in their addictive behavior. Breaking old patterns and routines is essential to breaking addictive behavior.

Pray Together

Praying over your children is an important part of being a parent. Sometimes when all else fails, the only thing you can do is turn to God for help. Moms and dads, teach your children how to pray. In their weakest moment, when your child feels alone and consumed by their addiction, they can reach out to God and talk to him about their problems. Oftentimes, it's our faith that keeps us hopeful throughout our trials because it anchors us and keeps us grounded so we don't get swept away by our problems. Spend time each day praying with your child. Speak words of affirmation and positivity over their lives, and hold their hands while you are manifesting a breakthrough. Prayer will also encourage your child by showing him that there is hope still, and that life is much more meaningful than their addictions.

Consult a Therapist or Addiction Specialist

If your teenager isn't responding to your efforts, there could be an underlying issue that needs to be addressed. Consider seeking help from a trained healthcare provider who will be able to assess your child and make a proper diagnosis. The majority of the time, teenagers fail to overcome their addictive behaviors because of a mental health issue such as depression. Treating the symptom will only help for a short while. You have to go down to the core of the problem and treat that first. As your child heals from their emotional and psychological pain, their addictive behaviors will subside as well. Parents often brush aside their teenager's cries for help because they think that they're just being dramatic. Please pay attention to your child and get them the help they need early.

In Closing

Addictive behavior is common in adolescence, but it has become even more prevalent in our modern world. Parents, don't beat yourselves up if your teenager has developed an addiction. Whether they're addicted to their gaming station or to drugs and alcohol, they have made a choice to engage in that behavior. Yes, they didn't know any better, but making these mistakes is how they're going to learn. As much as parents try to teach their children right from wrong, they still end up making their own decisions. What matters most is that you are there for them when they need you the most. Overcoming these addictions isn't easy, and your teenager will be extremely vulnerable during this time. Follow the tips provided in this chapter to offer guidance and support to your child so they can beat their addictions. Most of all, remember to show love and patience to your child, as this is the key to changing their mindset and opening their hearts.

Chapter 8:
Dealing With Conflict Constructively

Helping Your Teenager Manage Their Anger in Troublesome Situations

In this chapter, parents will come to understand the reason behind their teenager's bad temper, and they will learn critical skills about managing conflict which they can pass on to their teenage son. It's imperative that adolescent boys control their temper, or it could land them in hot water. This chapter has all the tips and tricks you need, as a parent, to calm your child down, and teach them alternative ways to express their intense emotions.

Teenage Boys Are Well-Known For Their Bad Temper

Boys will be boys! I'm sure you must have heard this saying one too many times as a parent. Every time you try to talk to a family member or friend about your son's bad temper, they always respond with that famous saying. It is true that teenage boys get into a lot of fights at school, and even in their community. Some of them carry weapons, such as pocket knives and knuckle busters, to school so that they can be prepared if anyone tries to start a fight. Boys tend to react impulsively in any situation. They rarely choose to think about things first before they react. What makes them this way? Why are boys quick to anger and violence? Why are they drawn to conflict? These are some of the questions parents ask themselves when they cannot understand their teenager's behavior. If you are of those parents, read on to find the answers you are looking for.

Teen Aggression

Have you been noticing a sudden change in your teenager's behavior? Is he angry and moody all the time? Does it seem like you have to walk on eggshells around your own home because you are scared that something you do or say might set off a tantrum in your teenage son? Teen aggression is a real emotional and psychological issue that many parents and teenagers battle with today. Parents are left dumbstruck when they come to learn of their teenager's getting involved in fights at school, hitting or punching their siblings, or even kicking the dog at home. These angry outbursts can cause a lot of damage to your teenager and to others, especially if they are faced with a conflict at any given time. Not all teenage boys develop teen aggression during adolescence. Some of them can keep their emotions under control and handle conflict without getting violent. Unfortunately, teens who do experience aggression often have a hard time keeping their emotions in check because they are overcome by intense anger. Parents, if you have tried everything you can to help your child, but their aggression still persists, then there could be an underlying issue fueling their anger and behavior issues.

ADHD/ADD

Teenagers who have ADHD/ADD, are more prone to developing teen aggression because of their impulsivity. They act on impulse without thinking about the consequences of their actions, which is why they get into fights so often. If your child has been diagnosed with ADHD/ADD, then this could be a core trigger for their aggressive behavior. If your child has not been diagnosed, consider taking them for a screening. Parents shouldn't throw in the towel so easily when it comes to their teenager's behavior issues because it could wreak havoc in their adult lives.

Substance Abuse

If your teenager has been involved in alcohol and drug use, this could very well be the reason behind their hostile and aggressive behavior. These substances alter the chemistry of the brain, resulting in changes in their mood, and affecting their ability to think clearly. Your teenager will seem more anxious and irritable than usual when they are unable to indulge in these substances, so if they are placed in a conflicting situation, they will resort to violence very easily. There will be times when your teenager gets involved in fights when they are under the influence of drugs and alcohol, and this happens because they cannot think clearly at that moment. As your child weans themselves off of these substances, you will notice a change in both their moods and demeanor.

Dealing With Physical or Sexual Abuse

Abuse is a topic that isn't spoken about enough when it comes to teenage boys. Parents avoid having this conversation with their teenage sons because they don't believe that adolescent boys are a target for sexual abuse. However, boys do experience both sexual and physical abuse in their lives. Bullies at school inflict physical abuse onto others, and your son may have been a target. Parents also beat their children out of anger, frustration, or because they are dealing with their own addictions. Whatever the abuse might be—sexual, emotional, or physical—it can have detrimental effects on a young man's confidence, for they would keep this a secret out of fear that they will be embarrassed. This can cause extreme emotional instability, which would then turn into anger and aggression.

Mood Disorders

Mental health disorders, such as bipolar disorder and anxiety disorder, cause a teenager to behave aggressively. Symptoms of these disorders might show up in early childhood, yet some parents brush them aside thinking that it's just a tantrum. When these disorders go untreated, they spiral out of control, especially during puberty when a teenager's hormones are all over the place. Once these mood disorders have been treated with the right medications, the aggression and anger subside over time. You will notice that your teen has become calmer and more conscious about his actions.

The Consequences of Poor Conflict Management

From ages 12 to 18, a teenager learns vital life skills which they carry with them for the rest of their lives. These life skills revolve around decision-making, hygiene and health, social relationships, education, and conflict management. If your child does not learn how to effectively manage and resolve conflict during this time, it will negatively affect their future in several ways. Parents sometimes brush away their teenagers' tantrums, aggressive behavior, and violent actions because they think that their children are still immature. However, this is the time when you are supposed to start treating your teenager as an adult to prepare them for the life they have to face when they become adults. Ignoring poor conflict resolution in your teenager will have dire consequences in their future. Let's take a look at some of the disadvantages of poor conflict management in teens.

Fraught Relationships With Friends and Family

Conflict is a part of life. Best friends fight amongst each other, parents argue with their children, siblings quarrel and disagree with one another over the littlest things, and neighbors sometimes exchange harsh words with each other. This is how normal relationships work. However, with the right conflict resolution skills, you can mend broken relationships and make them stronger. If your teenager does not understand how to do this, he will allow his anger to get the best of him. As long as he harbors resentment, and is willing to fight every chance he gets, he will never resolve any of the conflicts he faces. This will cause a disconnect from his friends and family, and these relationships will come undone as a result. It's important to go through life with the support of your parents, and your friends. But if you don't know how to live in harmony, you will be left alone.

Being Quick to Anger

Wearing your anger as a hat on your head will ensure that you fall into conflict frequently. If your teenager doesn't learn how to control his emotions, or how to handle stressful situations, he will always attract conflict wherever he goes. No matter how big or small the situation might be, your teenager will react with anger and he will lash out without thinking. People will be afraid to talk to him, or to raise a concern because they know that this person is going to argue and fight about every little thing. Your teenager won't be able to keep their anger in check just to keep the peace and to remain positive. Anger is one of the most detrimental emotions anyone could ever have. It blocks your ability to see things from another person's perspective, making it harder for you to grow as an individual. People make unforgivable mistakes when they are angry, and they often speak harsh words that ruin the lives of others, including their own.

The Risk of Landing Themselves in Jail

If your teenager gets into fights all the time at school, you should work on addressing this behavior. Violence against another should never be overlooked or tolerated because it becomes a way of life. Your teenager could very well land himself behind bars because of his inability to handle conflict using the correct methods. Poor emotional control, paired with aggressive behavior, equals a disaster waiting to happen. This is why so many teenage boys end up in jail. Their use of weapons like guns and knives, or beating someone up badly, or even killing someone will land them in prison. Sadly, this behavior is caused by their inability to handle conflict correctly. Parents, if you notice that your teenager is having difficulty controlling his emotions and he gets into fights all the time, then you need to get him help as soon as possible. The majority of the men in prison have had a poor upbringing, and they never learned key ways to control their anger. As the adult, you are responsible for your child's future. Pay attention to their behavior and take necessary action to help them become better human beings. I'm sure you don't want to see your child land in prison at any stage in their lives.

Failing to Keep a Stable Job

Keeping a job isn't easy, especially when they are millions of people waiting to take over your position. The workplace, undoubtedly, is a place where you find many conflicting opinions, as well as jealousy. Only the toughest survive, and they are able to keep their jobs because they can navigate themselves in difficult situations. If your teenager doesn't learn how to control his anger and find healthy ways to deal with conflict, he won't manage to keep his job for long. Soon, he will be hopping from job to job until he does enough damage to get himself a poor work record. Stability is extremely important career wise. If your teenager cannot keep his grades up in school because he is always getting into fights, then imagine what would happen later on in his work life. How will he work with others? How will he resolve situations where his co-workers or managers disagree with his opinion? A healthy work life requires a healthy attitude and mindset.

Strategies to Help Your Teen Deal With Conflict Effectively

Teenagers are young individuals who don't have a high level of maturity just yet. They react to situations differently because they see things from their level of understanding. This makes them quick to act, often without thinking about the consequences. Yes, it's normal for teenagers to get into trouble from time to time because they are still learning how to handle different situations in life. However, parents should make sure that they do whatever it takes to help their teenager make better choices for their future. Teenage boys will fight and disagree, and they might even throw some punches at one another. The important thing is that they understand the consequences that follow, and they are able to apologize and make the right decision the next time. Parents, here are a few great strategies that your teenager can try to build their conflict resolution skills.

Pay Attention to Your Emotions

Teenagers often fail to identify what emotions they are experiencing, especially when they are involved in a conflict with someone. Emotional awareness is key to understanding what you are feeling in that situation. Before you react, stop and pay attention to how you are feeling. Are you feeling angry? Or are you feeling offended or disrespected? Once your teenager has established how he is truly feeling, he can then truly understand himself. This way he can learn more about himself, and what his limits are. When teenagers don't recognize their emotions, they act out in ways that put themselves in danger, as well as others. Your teenager can try this 30 second trick to help them calm down and figure out what they are feeling at that moment.

- Close your eyes, take a nice, deep breath, and hold it for five seconds.

- Exhale slowly to allow all the tension to be released from your body.

- Pay attention to what you are feeling and think about what made you feel this way.

- Take another deep breath and hold for another five seconds.

- Exhale slowly, thinking about how you are going to react to the situation.

Listen Actively

An important aspect of successful conflict resolution is to pay attention and listen to what the other party has to say. Remember, they also have their own perspective on things, so they might not agree with you. Take the time to listen to how the other person is feeling, without interrupting them when they are talking. When you feel tempted to throw your opinion into the conversation, remind yourself that it's vital to understand the other person instead of arguing. Conflict gets out of control when people make assumptions and lash out at each other without making the effort to know the facts first. Listening is key to effective communication, and conflict can only be resolved with good communication between both parties.

Be Respectful

When conflict arises, people instantly forget their respect for one another. Because each person believes that they are right, they will stop at nothing to get their point across. They begin screaming and shouting at each other using vulgar languages, even becoming physically abusive towards one another. Teenagers won't think twice about being disrespectful towards another person, and they say exactly what's on their mind without thinking. Conflict can be handled well before it gets to the last stages, if only people can be respectful to each other. When your teenager is facing a conflict situation, encourage him to think about his words before he speaks. Explain to him how important it is to talk to others the way he wants to be spoken to. Screaming and speaking harsh words isn't going to solve the issue, but make it worse; however, respect can help you understand each other's perspective without hurting one another. Stay calm, even if the other person is being rude and shouting. Your calmness can be the key to defusing the bomb that is about to blow up. Your teenager must think about protecting their own peace at all costs, instead of making the situation worse.

Choose Your Battles Wisely

Not every argument or disagreement should take up all of your time and attention. Think clearly about whether this conflict is worth your time and effort before you jump right in. Teenagers must learn how to choose their battles wisely, or else they are going to find themselves getting into a lot of fights. Some arguments can be resolved by walking away and cutting off all energy from it. The more your teenager feeds into the drama, the worse their behavior is going to get. Picking and choosing which arguments are worth resolving is a daunting task, but it can save your teenager from making huge mistakes. Learning these critical skills early on in life gives your child an advantage you never had–to have control over your battles.

Think About the Relationship You Share With That Person

If your teenager gets into a fight with a friend or family member, it's crucial that they don't become lost in their rage and forget about their relationship with this person. Conflict is strong enough to break apart families and end year-long friendships. If adults cannot put aside their pride and prioritize their relationships above their petty arguments, then imagine how hard it would be for a teenager to do the right thing. If you start teaching your child that relationships hold a greater importance in life than conflict and disagreements, they will learn how to handle conflict with their close family and friends. Parents, you can break that chain of unhealthy conflict management that your mother or father may have passed on to you. Armed with the right knowledge, you can completely change your teenager's mindset to put people first, not arguments.

In Closing

The thing about conflict is that it can be very unpredictable. Your teenager could be chilling with his friends, having a pizza and talking about fast cars, and the next minute a fight breaks out, with everyone arguing and throwing fists at each other. How do you prepare your teenager for that situation? What do you think you could have done to avoid that from happening? The truth is, there is nothing you could have done to prevent conflict, and neither could your teenager. Conflict is inevitable. The only way you can handle it correctly is by changing your mindset and gaining more control over your emotions. Moms and dads, this is what you have to teach your child about. Controlling their emotions in the most difficult of situations will ensure that they remain calm enough to make the right decisions to resolve their arguments and disagreements constructively. It can be a real challenge to talk to your child about their behavior and about the choices they make. It's likely that they will respond with attitude, and they might even put a wall up and refuse to talk about it any further. But don't give up, mom and dad! This is an important aspect of your teenager's life, so find new ways to get your message across. Violence and swearing are never a solution to any problem, so help your teenager understand this early on in their lives, to save them from a future that could be ruined because of their anger and aggression.

Chapter 9
: Dating Advice and Lessons in Chivalry

How to Talk to Your Teenage Son About Dating and Being the Perfect Gentleman

In this chapter, parents will be encouraged to talk to their teenage sons about dating. Some moms might think that it's a bit too early to have this conversation; however, dads will understand why now is the right time! There are great tips for how your teenager can become a gentleman and treat girls with the utmost respect. Parents can also learn a thing or two on how to become chivalrous and keep abreast of the dating scene. Parents, the goal of this chapter is to help you raise a teenager who knows not only how to carry themselves well, but also how to behave with or around women. So, without further ado, let's get started!

The World of Dating for Teenage Boys

Yes, mom! Your son is finally old enough to have a girlfriend. Can you believe that? And dad, it's time for you to have that talk with your son about how to treat a lady. I understand, it's hard for any parent to accept that their child is no longer naive about the world around them. Their teenager has grown way beyond his years, and he no longer desires to participate in the childish activities he once enjoyed. Now, his interests lie in other things, like girls, for example. Once your son hits puberty, there are a gazillion things that are happening to his body. This also includes his hormones going off the charts, and his interests in girls growing along with it. In our modern world, the dating scene has changed quite a bit. In the past, teenagers weren't allowed to date until they were old enough and mature enough to understand how to be in a relationship with the opposite sex.

Boys weren't all that interested in girls because they were more intrigued by exploring the world, stealing their dad's car, and smoking weed in secret. Nowadays, their interests in girls have grown so much that boys aged 11 are already chatting to girls on social media and forming relationships with them. Parents, you have to adjust to the new world you're living in. Your teenage son, who just turned 13 a few days ago, is ready to date and explore his sexuality! This is the harsh reality parents have to face. The world of dating has completely changed for teenagers, and the only way parents can try to protect their children is to educate them as much as possible, and teach them how to be gentlemen who can treat women with respect, while gaining their respect in return.

The Truth About Teen Dating: It isn't All That Bad!

Believe it or not parents, but your teenager dating might not be such a bad thing. There are a few truths about dating which parents often fail to recognize because they're too focused on what their teenagers are doing, instead of what they're learning from the experience. Below, you will find four truths about dating that can actually help your teenager become more responsible and aware. Keep an open mind when reading through this section then you will be able to see these truths also.

Dating is Good For Building Relationship Skills

Teenagers often have a hard time connecting with others, especially when they are going through puberty and feeling insecure about themselves. Dating can actually help your teenager put himself out there and start building a network of friends through meeting different people and having actual conversations with them. It's okay to talk to people on social media because you don't have to actually see them face to face, and teenage boys become comfortable with that idea, until they're forced to dress up and go out to meet a girl they're interested in. This does incredible things for their self-confidence, and it helps them open themselves up to people easily. You can only build good people and relationship skills by actually spending time with others and talking about your lives. Hiding behind a phone isn't going to do much for your teenager's social life. The more dates your teenage son goes on, the more confident he will become. It's not guaranteed that he will have a perfect first date, but he will learn a lot from the process. He can pick up on social cues and watch the body language and facial expressions of girls to better understand them. This will help him extensively on his journey through dating.

Teenagers Open Their Eyes to the Reality of the Dating World

Dating isn't as romantic and exciting as the movies and music videos make it seem. Teenagers develop this idea of finding the perfect love and having the ultimate dating experience of a lifetime. However, when they try dating for themselves, they quickly realize how untrue their beliefs were. Dating during adolescence shouldn't be taken seriously because teenagers aren't mature enough to commit to another person at such a young age. When heartbreak hits, your teen son will come to understand that dating is difficult, and there is no such thing as the perfect romance. Entering into a relationship with unrealistic expectations only leads to disappointment. But when your teenager understands how dating really works, he will save himself from a lot of heartbreak and pain. It's good to believe in love, but he shouldn't become blind in it.

Your Teenager Discovers Who They Really Are

During puberty, teen boys struggle with their identity a lot. They are still learning more about themselves each day, which can be a frustrating process. Dating can play a huge role in helping your teenager learn new things about themselves. Meeting different people and getting to know them individually is good for discovering what you are looking for in a person. This way, your son will recognize what he is comfortable with, and what makes him upset. He will develop his own communication style and improve on his weaknesses. If your teenager is nervous when it comes to talking to girls, dating can help him overcome his fear, and turn his weakness into a strength. Just because your son is dating, it doesn't mean that he has to be sexually active. Dating involves getting to know others and getting to know yourself as well. When your teen is confident in who he is, he will flourish and grow in all aspects of life.

Teenagers Learn from Their Mistakes

Every parent will agree that their teenagers think they know it all, especially when it comes to dating and sex. As soon as they hear their parents talking about either one of these topics, they immediately turn a deaf ear, completely ignoring what their moms and dads have to say. What can you do when your teenager refuses to accept your advice? Leave them to make their own decisions so they can learn from their mistakes! Yes, it sounds a bit risky, especially when you think about your teenager making the wrong decisions when it comes to being sexually active. Moms and dads, you can offer as much advice as you can, talk until you're blue in the face, but your teenager is going to make their own decisions when the time comes. Your advice might help to guide them in the right direction, but they will have to choose their own path. The dating world isn't as easy as teenagers think. They will make a lot of mistakes, and many of their dreams will get crushed, but it will teach them valuable lessons. Teenagers can set healthy boundaries for themselves when dating, all thanks to the mistakes they made and lessons they learned.

Dating Advice for Your Teenage Son in the Era of Social Media

The time has finally come, moms and dads! Your little boy is now old enough to start dating. What advice could you possibly give to your son about dating in this new modern era of the internet and social media? Come to think of it, they probably know more than you do about the dating scene today. However, getting a bit of advice from a parent who comes from the "old fashioned" world of dating can be extremely helpful for your teenager. Just because he may know everything about the dating world today doesn't mean that it's a successful way of dating. This is why marriages don't last longer than a year nowadays, and most relationships barely survive past three months. The modern age has influenced the minds of people so deeply, that they don't understand what compromise means, or what going through the fire together is like. When the smallest argument crops up, both parties are ready to call it quits and go their separate ways. This kind of attitude of giving up and throwing in the towel then spreads to other areas of their lives as well. Parents, you need to teach your son how to remain true to his roots even though he is dating in the modern world. Here are some tips you can use to talk to your son about dating effectively in this day and age.

Don't Rely on Dating Apps

Dating apps have accelerated in popularity over the past few years, especially since Covid-19 forced the entire world into lockdown. During this time, people relied heavily on social media, dating apps, and messenger apps to connect with their loved ones and build new relationships with other people. This trend has now become the norm, as more and more youngsters prefer to date from the comfort of their own homes. Dating apps have evolved so much that people can match themselves up with a potential suitor just by uploading information about themselves. However, as convenient and easy as these dating apps can be, they also come with a lot of disadvantages. One of the main concerns is being able to trust the people you match up with on these apps.

Parents, advise your teens that people can be easily fooled by the biographies they come across on dating apps. Anyone can upload a fake picture of themselves and add fake information just to hook naive youngsters and trap them. Your teen son could fall head over heels in love with a girl on one of these dating apps, and they could be chatting for months, only for him to get his heart broken because he found out that this was a fake profile. These unforeseen situations make dating so unreliable and disappointing. Unfortunately, teenagers lose hope in dating because of this one negative experience. Parents should encourage their teenagers to seek more human contact when trying to date because this option is more reliable, and the experience is very different from online dating.

Be Cautious About the Information You Share Over Social Media

Teenagers love sending selfies and videos to their social media accounts for their friends and family to see. This has become the norm among youngsters these days, especially between teenagers who are dating. There isn't anything wrong with sharing a few pictures and videos with the person you are dating; however, the nature of those pictures and videos must be decent. Teen boys often exchange nude pictures with girls and share content that is of sexual nature. They send messages back and forth, make obscene videos, and send nude pictures thinking that they can trust the other person who is receiving this information. This is the worst thing any teenager, whether boy or girl, could do because it can backfire in devastating ways. Every parent should talk to their son about being a responsible, respectable boy who treats his own body, and that of others, with dignity. Not everyone can be trusted, not even the people your teenager might be dating, so he should never send any information that can be used against him in a defamatory manner. Your teenager should also respect the privacy of others. If he was sent messages and pictures of a sexual nature, it's best that he deletes them off his devices.

If Something Makes You Feel Uncomfortable, Don't Do It!

These days, teenagers have no clue what to do when it comes to dating. They don't take relationships seriously, they become bored quickly, and consequently, they start experimenting with their partners by trying new things. Your son must understand that he is NOT obligated to participate in anything he is not comfortable with. He has every right to say no to his partner, and he shouldn't feel guilty about it. Teen boys need to stop doing things just because everyone is doing it, and they should never force their partners into doing these things either. The dating culture of today is entirely different from the dating culture parents had in the past. Teenagers are now engaging in risky behavior that could land them in deep trouble. Parents, don't be afraid of talking to your son about standing up for himself when he is asked to do anything he isn't familiar with. He still has a long way to go in life, and a lot to learn in the process, so he can take things slow and do only what he is comfortable with.

Respect Each Other

Respect is of utmost importance between two people who are dating. When teenagers learn the importance of respecting others from a young age, they grow into responsible adults who can have successful relationships. As mentioned previously, conflict exists in every relationship. How your teenager chooses to handle this is entirely up to him. The foundation of every friendship and relationship is respect. It doesn't matter if your son is dating a girl for three days or three months– the level of respect should never decrease over time. Of course, this works both ways. There are many girls out there who don't understand what it means to respect boys, and the main reason for their disrespect is what they see on social media and what they have been taught by their parents. Women empowerment has taken a wrong turn in bad mouthing men and constantly pointing them out to be monsters. However, this isn't the case with all men. As long as your son understands how he should treat a lady, he wouldn't have anything to worry about. Respecting the boundaries that girls have are also very important. If they say "no," they mean "no," and teenage boys must take that seriously. As long as both parties have mutual respect for one another, then dating will be a great experience. We will take a deeper look at chivalry for teenage boys in the section below.

Chivalry for Teenage Boys

Every parent should strive to teach their boys to be respectful and courteous towards women, no matter how old they are. Women tend to believe that chivalry is dead in this new, modern age that we're living in, and they just might be right. Parents have lost the plot when it comes to teaching their boys about proper manners and etiquette. Here are a few tips that you can teach your son about being chivalrous in the twenty-first century.

- Say "please" and "thank you" when interacting with others.
- Always greet people with a smile wherever you go.
- Use appropriate table manners when sitting at the dinner table. This involves no talking with food in your mouth, no placing your elbows on the table, and always eating with a spoon or a fork.
- Offer to help out around the house with the chores, such as with the cooking, washing the dishes, or folding away the laundry.
- Always check if the other person is okay, especially when you can see that they're upset.
- Never use vulgar language around a girl and never raise your voice to instill fear in her.
- Always open the car door for a girl, especially if you're on a date.
- Offer to pay for the bill when you are out on a date. If she refuses many times, offer to split the bill instead.
- Always make sure that you drop a girl off home before midnight and that you keep to the promises you made to her parents.
- If there is a conflict to be settled, speak in a decent tone of voice and don't insult or degrade another person.
- Apologize when you have done something wrong and never let pride get the best of you.

In Closing

Dating is a new experience for a teenager, and the appropriate age a teenage boy should start dating is around 16-years-old. This is when they have a bit more understanding about the world around them and are able to think clearly. Your teen will need your advice and your support when he decides to start dating, so please don't make his experience horrible by hovering around him, or questioning him about every little thing. Yes, you should ask questions if there is a cause for concern, but other than that, let your teenager have this experience for himself. This chapter has given you all the information you need to guide your son in his dating life. That's all you can do as a parent–the rest is up to him! Trust your child that he will make the right choices because you have taught him well.

Chapter 10:
Bonding with Your Teenager

Four Amazing Bonding Activities for You to Do With Your Teenager

This short chapter aims to help parents bond with their teenagers on a whole new level. There are four key activities that parents can do with their sons to enhance closeness and build trust amongst the members of the family. These activities might take some getting used to, but the more you try, the better your chances of success!

1. Communication Building: Getting to Know One Another

Communication is the most important aspect of bonding as a family. Without it, each family member becomes estranged and secluded. This activity aims to promote healthy communication between parents and their children. It might take some time for your teenager to warm up to the idea of participating in activities, so be patient and supportive. Hang in there–don't give up just yet. Breakthrough is around the corner!

Instructions:

- Choose a quiet time to sit down with your teenager where there will be no disturbances.
- Each family member will need a pen and a paper.
- Next, everyone has to write three things on their own page about the other person that they like the most.
- Also write down three things that you would change about that person.
- Once this part of the activity is complete, take the time to agree that you all will listen actively and not interrupt when the other person is talking. Agree to be respectful and open to understanding everyone's perspective.
- Now, take turns reading out loud what you have written down. Try not to sound judgmental or insulting during the discussion.
- This exercise will help improve communication skills among family members.

2. Trust Building: Walking Blindfolded

Trust is another key aspect of building strong bonds with your teenager. Most children lose trust in their parents when they feel judged and criticized by them. This exercise will help moms and dads win back the trust of their children, while also creating an atmosphere of loyalty and honesty in the home.

Instructions:

- For this activity, you will have to place a blindfold over your teenager's eyes.
- Choose one parent who will guide your son around the house for approximately 15 minutes.
- This parent will help their teenager by giving directions and offering warnings to prevent them from tripping or stumbling into furniture.
- At the end of the 15 minutes, talk about the experience with your child, discussing how your teenager felt about being guided throughout the house with a blindfold on. Did he have faith in his parents?
- Now, switch roles and repeat the exercise. Both parent and child should be able to talk about their levels of trust in each other before and after the exercise.

Empathy Building: Appreciating Perspectives

It is quite hard to communicate experiences with family members, especially if these experiences are negative ones. There is a fear that the other person might not understand what you are feeling, and they might take it the wrong way. A quarrel that has taken place between a parent and child is an example of a negative situation that is hard to talk about.

In this case, empathy is required to see things from the other person's perspective.

Instructions:

- Find a quiet time of day to sit down with your teenager to carry out this exercise.
- You will need paper and pens for this activity.
- Make sure that you aren't sitting too close to each other because you will need a bit of privacy.
- Each of you will be required to write a poem about your feelings in regards to a particular situation which caused pain between the two of you.
- Read out your poems to each other, trying to listen patiently without interrupting.
- Try to see things from the other person's perspective, and at the end of the exercise, talk to each other about your feelings.

Bonding Exercise: Have Fun Together!

Taking the time out from a busy schedule is essential for bonding with your teenager. Most parents spend a lot of time working, tending to the home, and cooking meals that they have no time left to spend with their children. This makes your child feel abandoned and ignored, and the only way they know how to deal with these emotions is to shut themselves off from you. If you want to get through to your child, you have to break down those walls and start bonding again. Here's what you can do to bond with your teenager.

Father Bonding Activities

- Dads can take their sons on a fishing trip for the day. This is one of the most popular father and son activities around the world.

- If your son isn't into fishing, then you can plan an overnight camping trip somewhere nice. Boys usually love spending time outdoors.

- Teenage boys love playing sports. It would be a good idea to buy tickets to a soccer or baseball match, where you and your son can bond over the game.

- If you are on a tight budget dad, don't worry! A simple home barbeque can turn into a great bonding experience for you and your son. Cooking brings people together, so teaching your son how to get a barbeque started is a great idea to bring the family together.

Mother Bonding Activities

- Mom, you can plan a fun day of shopping and lunch with your teenage son. I know this might sound like an activity for girls, but boys love buying stuff too! You could go shopping for a new pair of takkies, or a new phone, whatever it is your child needs.

- If shopping is off the table, then you could go watch a movie together. Book tickets for a new movie your son wants to see, and plan a trip to the theater. Buy some popcorn and candy, whatever excites your teenager, and enjoy the movie

- Even though your son is a teenager, he still wants to lay down on your lap and rest while you play with his hair. This is the most intimate bonding experience between a mother and her child. Try this and watch how fast your son warms up to you again.

- Play a board game such as Scrabble or Monopoly with your son. Ask the other members of the family to join in as well. This is a great team building activity for the family.

In Closing

This chapter has provided you with examples of a few activities and exercises that you can make use of to bond with your teenager. It's vital that you keep an open mind when participating in these exercises, or you will unconsciously sabotage the bonding experiment with your negative mindset. Hype yourself up–make the experience fun for both you and your child! If you have a bored look on your face during any of these activities, your teenager will pick up on that, and he will lose interest in participating. It's your job to encourage him to keep trying because you know that it's for the good of your relationship with your son. These four short exercises have been designed to get you started on the road to having a better bond with your child. Nothing comes easy, so both you and your teenager must be willing to put in the work to build a better relationship. You can add on to this list of activities if you'd like, or you can create your own list that is more suitable for you and your teenager. Do whatever it takes to rebuild your broken relationship with your child as soon as possible because it's the only way that they are ever going to trust you again, especially now when they are going through a big phase in their lives.

Conclusion

What an incredible journey this has been, moms and dads! You have made it to the end of this guide–congratulations! I'm sure you have learned so much about your teenage son by now, and you probably see him through a different set of lenses now. While your son has grown up quite a bit, your job as a parent hasn't gotten any easier. In fact, it's gotten even more stressful! No need to worry though, because all your questions have been answered in great detail in this teenage parenting guide. In chapter one, we discussed everything about puberty, and how it impacts every area of your teenage son's life. You learned about the changes that take place, and how you can help your child through this process. In chapters two and three, we discussed the importance of practicing safe sex and the dangers of falling into bad friendships.

In chapters four and five, you discovered the importance of prioritizing your teenager's mental health, along with ways that you can help him boost his self-esteem as a young, vulnerable individual. Later on, in chapter six, we discussed the importance of school, and why it is crucial for teenage boys to have goals and dreams. In chapters seven and eight, you were alerted to the addictive behavior of your teenagers and learned new strategies to help them deal with conflict effectively. Finally, in chapters nine and ten, we explored the world of dating for teenagers, providing you with some amazing exercises to try with your teenager to rebuild trust, communication, love, and empathy.

This entire guide has truly opened your eyes to how vital your role as a parent is in the lives of your teenagers. We often think that our children are old enough to take care of themselves–to dress their own beds, make their own breakfast, do their own homework, and solve their own problems. While this is very true, to a certain extent, it doesn't mean that we should forget to check in with our children from time to time.

Parents, your teenager still needs you! He might not express this need in words, so pay attention to him, and do whatever you can to show him that you are still here no matter how old he gets. It's these little gestures, like making lunch and sending a sticky note saying "I love you," or dishing up a plate of food for your son, or kissing him on his forehead before he leaves for school, which remind your teenager that you still love him no matter what.

You are doing an outstanding job as a parent, so don't judge yourself too harshly! No one said that this journey would be easy, but you have made it this far without giving up. Have a little more faith in yourself and reward yourself, every now and then, for being a good parent. Your job as a parent isn't going to last very long! Soon, your teenager is going to be an 18-year-old man. He would have to take care of himself from then onwards, and you will finally get the time to live for yourselves. For now, spend as much time as you can with your son, making great memories together. This parenting guide will help you become the best parent you could ever be for your son. Apply all the family building exercises to your daily life, and you will definitely see a change soon! All the best on your journey, moms and dads! A bright future awaits both you and your teenager.

Thank you for choosing our guide to help you on your parenting journey! We hope that you have gained as much knowledge as you could from each chapter, and that you will apply the strategies you have learned to help your teenager become the best versions of themselves. If you enjoyed reading this book, please also consider reading the other books in our parenting teenagers collection. The covers of these books are shown below.

References

Cammarata, C. (2017). *About teen suicide (for Parents) - KidsHealth*. Kidshealth.org. https://kidshealth.org/en/parents/suicide.html

Centers, B. T. (2019, February 6). *Depression in teenage boys*. BNI Treatment Centers. https://bnitreatment.com/depression-in-teen-boys/#Signs_of_Depression_in_Teen_Boys

Goldman, R. (2015, December). *The stages of puberty: Development in girls and boys*. Healthline; Healthline Media. https://www.healthline.com/health/parenting/stages-of-puberty

Hailey, L. (2022, July 1). *31 Icebreaker games for teens for any situation*. Science of People. https://www.scienceofpeople.com/icebreakers-for-teens/

HIV.gov. (2020, June 15). *What are HIV and AIDS?* HIV.gov. https://www.hiv.gov/hiv-basics/overview/about-hiv-and-aids/what-are-hiv-and-aids

Staff, Familydoctor Org Editorial, & jswords. (2017, January 4). *Boys and puberty*. Familydoctor.org. https://familydoctor.org/boys-and-puberty/#:~:text=Changes%20to%20emotions%20and%20thinking

Top 25 goal quotes (of 1000). (n.d.). A-Z Quotes. https://www.azquotes.com/quotes/topics/goal.html

Tripp, P. (2019, March 19). *How do I talk with my kids about sex?* Www.paultripp.com. https://www.paultripp.com/ask-paul-tripp/posts/how-do-i-talk-with-my-kids-about-sex?

Image References

Alderson, D. (2021, March 3). *People tossing their drinks in celebration* [Photograph]. Pexels.com. https://www.pexels.com/photo/people-tossing-their-drinks-in-celebration-of-the-holiday-7016492/

Cottonbro Studio. (2020, October 21). *People drinking beer* [Photograph] Pexels.com. https://www.pexels.com/photo/people-drinking-beer-beside-the-brick-wall-5531897/

Cottonbro Studio. (2020a 28). *Person holding a contraceptive* [Photograph] Pexels.com. https://www.pexels.com/photo/person-holding-a-contraceptive-5713044/

Cottonbro Studio. (2020b, July 24). *Person in blue denim jeans and white sneakers* [Photograph] Pexels.com. https://www.pexels.com/photo/person-in-blue-denim-jeans-and-white-sneakers-4858872/

Cottonbro Studio. (2021a, March 24). *Photo of boys fighting* [Photograph] Pexels.com. https://www.pexels.com/photo/photo-of-boys-fighting-7243958/

Cottonbro Studio. (2021b, March 24). *Young men smoking together* [Photograph] Pexels.com. https://www.pexels.com/photo/young-men-smoking-together-7244451/

Cottonbro Studio. (2021c, March 25). *A shirtless boy with shaving cream on their face* [Photograph] Pexels.com. https://www.pexels.com/photo/a-shirtless-boys-with-shaving-cream-on-their-face-7253880/

Grabowska, K. (2020, December 22). *Boy standing in front of a blackboard* [Photograph] Pexels.com.

https://www.pexels.com/photo/boy-standing-in-front-of-a-blackboard-with-an-equation-written-on-it-6256110/

Hossler, B. (2022, August 19). *A man in a blue graduation gown* [Photograph] Pexels.com. https://www.pexels.com/photo/a-man-in-blue-graduation-gown-13276891/

Khan, I. (2018, June 5). *Man in black shirt and gray pants* [Photograph] Pexels.com. https://www.pexels.com/photo/man-in-black-shirt-and-gray-denim-pants-sitting-on-gray-padded-bench-1134204/

Koolshooters. (2021, January 20). *Man-love-people-woman* [Photograph] Pexels.com. https://www.pexels.com/photo/man-love-people-woman-6621883/

Kozik, A. (2022, March 8). *Letter tiles and leaves on a pink page* [Photograph] Pexels.com. https://www.pexels.com/photo/letter-tiles-and-leaves-on-a-pink-background-8326282/

Krukau, Y. (2021, August 5). *A man playing a video game* [Photograph] Pexels.com. https://www.pexels.com/photo/a-man-playing-a-video-game-in-a-computer-9071739/

Media, K. (2021a, June 30). *Man in pink shirt sitting beside teenager* [Photograph] Pexels.com. https://www.pexels.com/photo/man-in-a-pink-shirt-sitting-beside-a-teenager-crying-8550682/

Media, K. (2021b, June 30). *Woman in blue shit talking to a young man* [Photograph] Pexels.com. https://www.pexels.com/photo/woman-in-blue-shirt-talking-to-a-young-man-in-white-shirt-8550841/

Son, H. (2022, July 19). *Standing teenager boys wearing school uniforms* [Photograph] Pexels.com.

https://www.pexels.com/photo/standing-teenager-boys-wearing-school-uniforms-12885699/

Thomas, J. (2018, September 11). *Man giving jacket to woman* [Photograph] Pexels.com. https://www.pexels.com/photo/man-giving-jacket-to-woman-1405739/

Wilcox, K. (2018, April 1). *Four men sitting on the platform* [Photograph] Pexels.com. https://www.pexels.com/photo/four-men-sitting-on-platform-923657

www.ingramcontent.com/pod-product-compliance
Lightning Source LLC
Chambersburg PA
CBHW070307010526
44107CB00056B/2512